Mustang

First published in 2006 by Motorbooks, an imprint of MBI Publishing Company, Galtier Plaza, Suite 200, 380 Jackson Street, St. Paul, MN 55101-3885 USA

MBI Publishing Company titles are also available at discounts in bulk quantity for industrial or sales-promotional use. For details write to Special Sales Manager at MBI Publishing Company, Galtier Plaza, Suite 200, 380 Jackson Street, St. Paul, MN 55101-3885 USA

ISBN-13: 978-0-7603-2556-8
ISBN-10: 0-7603-2556-1

Editor: Peter Schletty
Designer: Maria Friedrich

Printed in China

On the cover: The 1969 Mach 1 required a larger engine compartment for the 428-cubic-inch plant rumbling under the Shaker hood scoop.

On the frontispiece: This galloping stallion has signified Mustang power and speed for over 40 years.

On the title pages: The 2006 GT was voted America's Best Muscle Car by *Car and Driver*, and with 320 lb-ft of torque and live rear axle for smooth handling, it's easy to see why.

On the back cover:
Left: The 1970 Mach 1 featured the debut of the powerful 300-horsepower Cleveland engine as a $48 optional upgrade.

Middle: The Roush Mustang Stage III convertible carries an Eaton supercharger atop a 4.6L V-8 beefing up the quarter-mile time to 13.56 seconds at 104.80 miles per hour.

Right: The 2006 GT recalls classic Mustang lines, low profile, and sharp grille. A 4.6L, 300-horsepower V-8 lurks under the hood.

Author Bio

Acclaimed photographer David Newhardt lives in Pasadena, California. His work includes writing and photography for books such as *Mustang: 1964 ½–1973*, and *Firebird Trans Am*, photography for *Mopar Muscle: Fifty Years*, *Shelby Mustang: Racer for the Street*, *Mustang: Forty Years* and many more.

Contents

Introduction

Mustang Gallery

Few people had any inkling that the Mustang was going to be the biggest hit in the automotive market in the postwar era. The core development team at Ford, including Lido "Lee" Iacocca, wanted to put out an inexpensive "secretary's car," using mechanical components from the humble Falcon. In the Mike Mueller book *Mustang 1964 ½–1973*, former product planning manager Don Frey recalls, "We started watching registrations of the Corvair, which was a dog. I guess in desperation they put bucket seats in the thing, called it a Monza and it started to sell. We got the idea that there must be something to it. And that's how it all started, watching Monzas."

Iacocca was promoted to vice president and general manager of Ford Division with the departure of imaginationally-challenged Robert McNamara, and was determined to take advantage of the maturing postwar baby boomers. This group was born relatively free from want, raised by a generation that survived through the Great Depression and World War II. The boomers held the purse strings on the largest amount of disposable income the world had ever seen. Because of their huge numbers and their growing desire to enjoy life to the fullest, in hindsight it was a no-brainer to pursue them.

However, many senior automobile executives cut their teeth in another era, and they failed to realize that a real car-buying revolution was on the rapidly approaching horizon. Iacocca, then in his 30s, brought a perspective to the planning process that was missing. Now with his ascension to high office, he started the wheels moving towards creating an affordable, fun-lifestyle vehicle. And he wanted it yesterday.

Iacocca handed the assignment to Don Frey and his assistant Hal Sperlich. As Randy

Leffingwell and Darwin Holmstrom recall in their book, *Muscle: America's Legendary Performance Cars*, "Frey and Sperlich were charged with creating a 'special Falcon,' a sporty 2+2-seat car (a car with minimal rear seats) based on the Falcon chassis. The car was to cost no more than $2,500 and weigh no more than 2,500 lbs."

Just because the title of vice president was on Iacocca's door didn't mean that his wish became law in Dearborn. The big guy, Chairman Henry Ford II, wasn't sold on the concept, and he made no secret of his reluctance to repeat the Edsel debacle. In meeting after meeting, "The Deuce" shot down the proposal. It was only after the fifth meeting that Ford approached Frey and said that he would give permission to build the car—but if it failed, it was Frey's neck.

As events would bear out, Iacocca had his finger firmly on the pulse of the youth market, and when the Mustang debuted on April 17, 1964, huge sheets of paper were torn off of showroom windows to allow the public the chance to see the new automobile that had been enjoying an unprecedented advertising campaign. To say that the public was taken with the new offering would be a gross understatement, as more than 22,000 units were sold on the *first day*! By the end of the first full year's production, an amazing 418,812 Mustangs had rolled out of showrooms.

Ford's competitors were caught flatfooted. Plymouth had introduced their Barracuda two weeks *before* the Mustang, but except for a fastback greenhouse, it differed little from the Valiant it was based on. The youth market yawned at the Barracuda much the same way they yawned at the Valiant. It would take Chevrolet two years to rush the Camaro into production. By then, the Mustang was firmly entrenched as *the* car for the young and young at heart.

Since he had started at Ford, Iacocca realized that performance could sell automobiles. When his hour of power arrived, he instituted a program called Total Performance, a two-pronged assault on the racetrack and showroom. It was one thing to earn wins on Sunday, but if it couldn't be translated into sales on Monday, then the entire effort was moot. Iacocca made sure that customers had the chance to live out their Walter Mitty fantasies behind the wheel of a high-performance Ford, and the Mustang was the tip of the spear. With the installation of the high-revving 289-ci V-8 and a four-barrel carburetor, the K-code was born, and automotive enthusiasts used the Mustang as the yardstick from that day forward.

As the 1960s slid by, the Mustang grew, both in stature and size. Competition in the pony and muscle car market was heating up, and the easiest way to keep the Mustang in front was to slip in yet more horsepower. Often, this was done in the American fashion, by getting a bigger hammer. Cubic inches were rising faster than a Saturn V rocket, and as the

Sixties came to a close, the power output of some of these engines was staggering. Yet the bubble was destined to pop. Government, working with environmentalists, crafted regulation that would work towards reducing pollution from automobiles. Unfortunately, the technology in Detroit was not up to the task, and in an effort to fulfill the letter of the law, performance disappeared faster than a politician's promise. Unleaded gasoline came on the scene, and all of the auto makers struggled to instill even a whiff of performance. The Mustang downsized, both in dimensions and power output.

While the Mustang II didn't have the visceral excitement of Mustangs from a handful of years before, they kept the nameplate alive. Some competitors weren't as lucky, as the Barracuda and Challenger bowed out of the market. The public snapped up hundreds of thousands of the little Fords, and as technology slowly progressed, a new platform, the Fox, became the recipient of these improvements. The Mustang was on the verge of a renaissance.

By the time the 1980s rolled into view, computers started becoming standard under the hood of automobiles, and the advantages were many. While shade-tree mechanics could no longer tinker with the engine on weekends, power was steadily returning to the engine compartment of the Mustang, along with cleaner emissions and improved fuel economy. The long-lived 5.0-liter V-8 was the standard bearer for Mustang performance, Ford engineers' efforts to restore muscle under the hood was paying off. They even developed

non-musclecar traditional powerplants, including turbocharging. Yet as the Eighties came to a close, Mustang performance was spelled V-8, again.

Occasional stylistic freshening and frequent injections of horsepower kept the Mustang on the enthusiast's radar screen as the 1990s started, and as the decade passed, power levels and fuel economy rose. The Cobra name returned with real venom. These limited-production models kept the public interested in the Mustang, and showed that real motorheads were working to keep the Mustang at the top of the hill. Many of them could generate performance numbers that would embarrass the mighty Mustangs from the 1960s while keeping occupants comfortable with air conditioning. All while delivering fuel economy 250 percent better.

Now a new generation of Mustang has hit the road, delivering unrivaled performance at an incredible price point. The new design recalls some of the historic Mustangs, yet it is creating a heritage of its own. A new Shelby Mustang is on the verge of Job #1, and with record horsepower it promises to weave a significant piece of history into the fabric that is the Mustang.

Competing automakers have seen the wisdom of a high-profile, fun, affordable, youth-targeted vehicle and are bringing back such storied nameplates as Challenger and Camaro. The formula is as valid today as it was in 1964.

1964-1966

Chapter 1

I n late 1964, no one anticipated the clamor Ford's new mid-engine car would create. Nobody expected such strong, positive reactions. The Mustang accomplished something for Ford Motor Company that no other Ford division car had done in several years: it provided favorable enthusiast publicity. That recognition went to Iacocca.

Between mid-October and early November, magazine and newspaper writers and photographers kept the car visible. The Mustang got cover play on the December issues of the major and minor auto magazines. The most recent Ford-powered product to garner that kind of attention had been just nine months earlier when Carroll Shelby's Cobras had caught the eyes and hearts of car magazine writers and editors. But that, Iacocca knew, was Shelby's car, not his. Now he had an accomplishment he could point to that was achieved under his tenure. However, it was exactly what he didn't want: a wildly favorable reaction to a two-seater.

Several of the engineers involved in the project took the Mustang on tour across the United States. It starred in major auto shows from New York to Los Angeles, and after the big shows, it began a college tour. On one run alone, they visited 17 universities where there were mechanical or automotive engineering schools and student chapters of the Society of Automotive Engineers (SAE). Ford printed 30,000 brochures and its engineers gave away every one. On occasion they showed up with the car unannounced, just to gauge spontaneous reaction, driving it onto college campuses from coast to coast. It created traffic jams. Crowds constantly, and sometimes instantly, mobbed the car. Ford engineering took advantage of the frenzy and used the Mustang to recruit top engineering candidates to come to work for Ford. Everywhere the engineers traveled with the Mustang, people wanted to know when it would be available and how much it would cost.

By that time, however, Iacocca had been making it clear the car would not be produced.

He recognized its image value, though, and in public he characterized it as something "to show the kids that they should wait for us because we had some good, hot stuff coming."

Because the Mustang functioned so well, it thrilled the magazine writers and photographers. Chevrolet introduced its Corvair Monza GT during the same Grand Prix weekend. While GM employees pushed their show car from one display area to the next, the Mustang ran laps as the official pace car for the race. Lunn's group later assembled a second Mustang made of fiberglass. It did not have an engine/transaxle and it was only a push-around model for auto-show static displays.

While the mid-engine Mustang had been in the works, around mid-1962, Iacocca had proposed to Henry Ford II a new car program that would produce a four-seater based on what he'd seen in Bordinat's studios. He had received a cool reception. Iacocca's Falcon Sprint had failed to meet its sales expectations, in part because its sale price came in about $600 higher than the Corvair Monza, even though it had fewer standard features. Ford dealers couldn't give them away, nor would they stop screaming about it. For Henry Ford II, the idea of committing corporate funds now to a new four-passenger sporty-car seemed ill-advised.

The foundation of the production car, still called the Cougar or referred to by its in-house code designation as the T-5, basically was the Falcon Sprint. Nothing invented for Roy Lunn's Mustang would be carried over into production. That technology would go elsewhere with Lunn, and later with Negstad and others to England and on into racing.

To produce a working, running Mustang in such a short time period meant borrowing parts and ideas from somewhere else. For years, Detroit Steel Tube (DST) had done custom fabrication and modification for Ford Motor Company to prepare prototype cars for evaluation and modeling purposes. Ford engineering had already asked them to put the new Fairlane 221-ci V-8 into the Falcon. It became the Falcon Sprint, an evolution that had required countless other modifications.

Narrow bias-ply tires were state of the art in 1964 when the Mustang debuted.

This Wimbledon White Mustang was the first one off the production line. It was sold to an airline pilot, then he traded it to Ford two years later for the one millionth Mustang built.

Sporty, fresh and able to seat four, the twin-cockpit design targeted the young and young at heart.

Price (base convertible): $2,557.64

Engine: 260-ci V-8, 164-horsepower

Transmission: 4-speed manual

Total early-1965 convertible production: 28,833

With sales of 22,000 units sold on April 17, 1964, the Mustang debuted to a public hungry for a sporty, affordable family car. By the time the 1965 model year was finished, Ford had sold an amazing 680,989 units. Not bad for a car that used the modest Falcon as its mechanical base, over which was fitted the swoopy body styled by Joe Oros' design team.

When the Mustang debuted, it was available in two configurations: convertible and hardtop. With a base price of $2,320.96, the Mustang hardtop was a canvas that an arm-long option list could transform into a grocery getter, a street brawler, or anywhere in between. This was the genius of Lee Iacocca's marketing plan.

Price (base hardtop): $2,320.96, (originally sold in Canada)

Engine: 170-ci, 101-horsepower, U-code inline six cylinder

Transmission: 3-speed manual

Total early-1965 hardtop production: 92,705

This model has a 170-ci straight six-cylinder engine and a manual transmission.

Tri-element taillights have been used on the Mustang during its entire life.

Long front fenders hid the Mustang's Falcon roots. Simple, crisp lines have been a Mustang hallmark since Day One.

Price: Given to Ford dealers

Engine: 260-ci, 164-horsepower, F-code V-8

Transmission: 3-speed automatic

Total production: 190 hardtops, 35
  convertibles

Each of the 190 hardtop and 35 convertibles fitted out as streetable Pace Car replicas were painted Pace Car White (paint code C) and came equipped with a 164-horsepower, 260-ci V-8 and an automatic transmission. The three actual Pace Cars used at the Brickyard were finished in Wimbledon White (paint code M), and were fitted with the 289-ci "Hi-Po" V-8, mated to a Borg-Warner 4-speed manual transmission.

Designer Phil Clark drew the galloping horse logo that would visually define the new sporty car from Ford.

Early in the Mustang's production, the 164-hp 260-ci V-8 was replaced by the 289-ci engine.

The 1965 Pace Car replica celebrated the Mustang's role as Pace Car at the 48th annual Indianapolis 500-mile race. Dealerships winning Ford's "Checkered Flag" contest were awarded a Pace Car replica.

Price: $6,047 (for off-road use only)

Engine: 289-ci, 350-horsepower, R-code V-8

Transmission: 4-speed manual

Total production: 36

In an effort to lighten the GT350R, the interior was stripped down to metal. This had the secondary effect of "fireproofing" the cockpit. Further weight reduction included the removal of front and rear bumpers, replacing door glass with Plexiglas and fashioning a gas tank from two regular Mustang fuel tanks sliced in half and welded together. The R-model cost $1,500 more than the $4,547 needed for a regular Shelby GT-350.

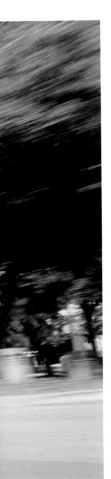

Only 36 Shelby GT350Rs were built, all destined for the racetrack. With 350 horsepower on tap, the R-model dominated the B/Production class. Legend has it that Carroll Shelby had a coworker pace off the distance between two buildings to come up with the "350" designation.

To minimize pressure build-up in the interior and separation of the window from the vehicle at race speeds, the Plexiglas rear window incorporated a vent at the top.

Only one transmission was available with the K-Code option—a four-speed manual. The K-code option ran through 1966, when big-block engines delivered prodigious torque for less money.

With a solid-lifter 271-horsepower, 289-ci V-8 under the long hood, the 1965 K-Code Mustang was the hottest one in the catalog. The 480-cfm Autolite carburetor fed the 10.5:1 compression ratio cylinders with Premium fuel.

A well-driven K-code Mustang could cover the quarter-mile in 15.9 seconds, while a 0-60 mph time of 7.6 seconds bested the GTO. Unlike the standard 8-inch rear axle ring gear, the K-code used a 9-inch unit, the better to hold up under the increased power the high-revving small-block generated. Buyers had to pay an additional $327.92 for the K-code engine without the GT Equipment Group option, or $276.34 with the option.

Price (fastback with GT Equipment Group): $2,809.53

Engine: 289-ci, 271-horsepower, K-code V-8

Transmission: 4-speed manual

Total fastback production: 77,079

Price: $544.13 over $2557.64 base
   convertible price

Engine: 289-ci, 225-horsepower, A-code V-8

Transmission: 4-speed manual

Total convertible production: 101,949

Most buyers in 1965 desiring Mustang performance sprang for the healthy A-code. With 225 horsepower, it was $52.85 over the price of the 200-horsepower V-8 and was money well spent. It could be equipped with either a manual or automatic transmission. All V-8 powered Mustangs used five-lug wheels, and all V-8 engines were painted black with gold air cleaners and valve covers.

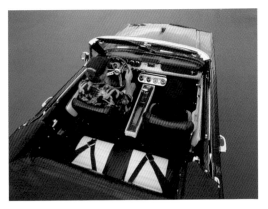

More accurately a 2+2 rather than a true four-seater, the 1965 Mustang convertible let everyone work on their tan while cruising in style.

Only 9.1 percent of buyers bought air conditioning, a $277.20 option.

The GT Equipment Group option included rocker stripes, fog lamps in the grille, quick ratio steering, and the Special Handling Package.

Price: $4,547

Engine: 289-ci, 306-horsepower, K-code V-8

Transmission: 4-speed manual

Total production (street models): 516

Under the fiberglass hood lurked a 289-ci V-8 the Shelby's crew had massaged with tried and true hot rod tricks, such as mounting a 715-cfm Holley four-barrel carburetor atop a cast-aluminum Hi-Riser intake manifold, and fitting Tri-Y steel headers and Glaspak mufflers. The result was 306 honest horsepower. The 1966 Shelby GT350 routed the exhaust pipes to the rear of the car, in order to "civilize" it for more mainstream tastes.

In order to correct a large blind spot, the louvers in the C-pillar were replaced with Plexiglas windows.

Discrete badging at the rear of the GT350 was an interesting visual balance to the twin, full-length stripes worn by most Shelby Mustangs.

The classic long hood and short trunk proportions were part of the reason the Mustang and its Shelby version were such a hit with the public.

Price: Negotiated with race team owners

Engine: 289-ci, 350-horsepower V-8

Transmission: 4-speed manual

Total production (Group 2): 16

Group 2 Mustangs were prepared by Shelby to GT350R specs, with the exception of window glass and a full interior. Sixteen Group 2 1966 Mustangs were built, and like regular R-model Shelbys, the Shelby American racing 289-ci engine generated approximately 360-horsepower. In order to access the 34-gallon fuel tank, the pinned trunk lid had to be opened.

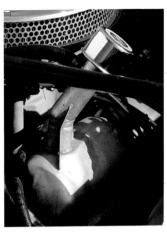

Above: With the exception of the SCCA-mandated full roll cage and racing harnesses, the interior was stock.

Below: This 1966 Group 2 coupe was built for Shelby driver Ken Miles to compete in the Trans Am series, but before he had a chance to drive it, he was killed at Riverside Raceway on August 17, 1966, testing a GT40 prototype.

R-Model engines were used in the Group 2 Mustangs, including balancing and blueprinting it to generate more power as well an allowing it to survive on the racetrack. As the vehicle was not intended for street use, a breather on each valve cover vented crankcase pressure to the atmosphere.

Stylist Peter Brock came up with the idea of rocker panel stripes, a design element that many have copied. Most GT350Hs were equipped with automatic transmissions in the belief that the vehicles wouldn't be "abused" as much.

The scoops in front of the rear wheels were functional, feeding cool air to the rear brakes. The vents in the C-pillar of the 1965 GT350 were replaced with Plexiglas to improve visibility.

For $17 a day and 17 cents a mile, anyone older than 25 with a good driving record could live out those Walter Mitty dreams of driving a race car by going to a participating Hertz Rent-A-Car location and grabbing the keys. The 1,000 vehicles that Hertz ordered made up about 40 percent of Shelby's business in 1966.

Price: Negotiated with Hertz management

Engine: 289-ci, 306-horsepower V-8

Transmission: 3-speed automatic, 4-speed manual

Total production: 1,000

The vast majority of 1965 Mustang GTs were equipped with a 225-horsepower, 289-ci V-8. Rocker stripes were part of a $165.03 GT package. The C-line running down the side was meant to evoke the functional air scoops found on the original Mustang I concept car from 1962. Mustangs equipped with a V-8 engine sported a small "V" badge on the front of the front fender.

Price (base hardtop): $2,320.96

Engine: 289-ci, 225-horsepower, A-code V-8

Transmission: 4-speed manual

Total production: 22,232

While Mustangs equipped with the GT Equipment Package used disc brakes on the front, the rear tires depended on drum brakes to shed velocity.

The GT featured a special upholstery option with embossed stallions in the leather. *Photo courtesy of Mike Mueller*

Neat and tidy. These were the days when the entire engine was visible, even with a 289-ci V-8.

The Interior Décor Group option included a deluxe woodgrain steering wheel and dash insets. Padded sun visors became standard in 1966.

For 1966, the side trim behind the doors was changed. It was an inexpensive way to freshen a new model.

Price (base hardtop): $2,416.18

Engine: 289-ci, 200-horsepower, C-code V-8

Transmission: 3-speed automatic

Total hardtop production: 499,751

Ford knew better than to mess with success, and with massive sales the year before, change was limited to some trim and bright work. Sales didn't suffer, as 607,568 vehicles went to happy homes. Base price on a hardtop was only $2,416.18.

A center console with air conditioning went for $31.52. It cost $310.90 for the air conditioning system.

Bias ply tires on 14-inch wheels were the norm on Mustangs in 1966.

With a 9.2:1 compression ratio and hydraulic lifters, the 200-ci straight six found in the 1966 Mustang Sprint developed 120 horsepower at 4,400 rpm.

Price (base hardtop): $2,416.18

Engine: 200-ci, 120-horsepower, T-code inline six

Transmission: 3-speed automatic

Total standard hardtop production: 422,416

For the Mustang buyer on a budget, Ford offered the Sprint model, a minimal frills pony car. Though fuel economy was not as integral a part of the auto buying experience as it is today, stretching a gallon appealed to many, even with 25-cent-per-gallon gasoline.

1966 SHELBY GT350 DRAG RACER

Shelby built nine drag cars in 1965 and four in 1966, including this example, #6S011. Stock 15-inch wheels were surrounded by Casler "cheater slicks" in 1966, and the exhaust was routed out in front of the rear wheels, similar to 1965 GT350s.

Price: Negotiated with race team owners

Engine: 289-ci, 306-horsepower, K-code V-8

Transmission: 4-speed manual

Total production: 4

The tall hood scoop was designed to ingest large quantities of cool air and ram it into the Holley carburetor. Gus Zuidema of Lebanon Valley, New York, covered the quarter-mile in 12.68 seconds in a factory drag car.

Externally, the Shelby factory drag car looked like a stock 1966 GT350, but a wealth of improvements under the skin allowed the vehicles to be highly competitive. Belanger drag headers were designed for this brutal environment.

1967-1970

Chapter 2

A s the Mustang entered the late Sixties, it did what many people do as they get older: it got bigger. It retained the same wheelbase as the original Mustang, but the body grew in all dimensions to allow Ford's engineers to slip ever more powerful motors under the long hood. Part of Lee Iacocca's Total Performance package was Ford's pursuit of racetrack victories, and often, race sanctioning organizations required a street-legal version of a race car. Ford Motor Company lived by the adage, "Win on Sunday, Sell on Monday," and its string of victories were testament that it knew how to win on Sunday.

Ford introduced the Mustang to the big-block format in 1967 with a 390-ci V-8, but this engine was a trifle tame compared with the large displacement/large power engines from GM. Yet it pointed in the direction Ford would have to take to increase power and sales. The old saying "there's no substitute for cubic inches" would guide the development of the Mustang for the next handful of years.

In mid-1968, a new engine, the Cobra Jet, was introduced, made up of components on Ford's shelves. It was a success, and paved the way for increased grunt in the Mustang. The first 50 built were identical, stripped, consecutive VIN vehicles that were funneled to drag racers, who put the light weight and high power to good effect. This fit into Ford's desire to be a dominant force in a wide range of racing. Lessons learned from the generation of the Cobra Jet program were carried into next performance offerings.

Still offered were six-cylinder models, ideal for daily commutes, but the buff book ink was spilled on vehicles like the Boss series and Cobra Jets. Two Boss engines, the 302-ci V-8 aimed at the Trans Am series, and the 429-ci V-8, released to allow Ford to use the engine in NASCAR, were little more than barely street-legal race motors. Ironically, the Boss 429 found success on the drag strip rather than on superspeedway ovals, but its low production numbers meant that seeing one on the street was a rare event. It literally overflowed the engine compartment, requiring the crew at

Kar Kraft to wield hammers to "modify" the front shock absorber towers to shoehorn in the massive engine. The Boss 302 competed with victories on the Trans Am circuits, yet it too had low sales figures. But it was fulfilling the Ford corporate edict of bringing home the trophies.

The real star in the 1969 Mustang lineup was the new Mach 1, which could be outfitted to cater to any buyer's tastes. Though it never competed in a sanctioned race series, the Mach 1 was a winner where it mattered to the corporation: the bottom line. It could be equipped with engines ranging from the standard 351-2V V-8 to the brutal 428-ci Super Cobra Jet. With its blacked-out hood and SportsRoof silhouette, it racked up big sales. Customers could *look* the part of Speed Racer, without the hassle of indulging in actual anti-social behavior. Hence the public bought a *lot* of Mach 1s, eclipsing the Boss series in profile and sales. The lesson was not lost on the decision makers in Dearborn: when in doubt, give the suggestion of performance, not always the real thing.

This isn't to say that a suitably equipped Mustang couldn't waste a set of rear tires with the best of them. The Boss 429, using a huge, functional hood scoop to feed gobs of fresh air to an undersized carburetor and a restrictive exhaust system, still had more torque on tap than any street tire made could handle. With its understated graphics, it wasn't hard for someone to ignore it at a stop light. That usually happened just once.

When the road filled with curves, the Boss 302 would handily embarrass many "proper" sports cars. Sporting a graphics package designed by Larry Shinoda, it looked the part of a Trans Am car that wandered onto the street. However, unlike a lot of wannabe street racers, the Boss 302 could walk the walk. Its 302-ci V-8 lived to spin, and it needed an electronic rev-limiter to keep the internal parts internal. Laughably under rated at 290 horsepower, it actually generated a reliable 350 horsepower in a lightweight package, ideal for the twists and turns of street "competition."

For the buyer that embraced the extroverted persona of the Mach 1, it could be transformed into a brutal straight-line stormer by ordering either the Cobra Jet engine, or the drag-strip specific Super Cobra Jet option, built for covering the quarter-mile (or running to the next stop light) in crushing fashion.

When the 1970 models rolled into the showrooms, the freshening of the sheet metal was apparent, as was the continued performance slant. General Motors and Chrysler had thinly disguised race cars with license plate frames available at their dealers, and Ford was determined to match them horsepower for horsepower. The same engine options that made 1969 such a performance bonanza were offered for 1970. The result was a high-water mark in American performance vehicles. Mach 1, Boss 302, and Boss 429 were on the lips of automobile enthusiasts, even if they drove something else.

People with their ear on the rail were aware that looming governmental regulations were going to put the brakes on the performance bandwagon. Anyone with a wit of knowledge grabbed a performance Mustang while they could. While the regulation ax would take a couple of years to fully descend, it was on its inevitable path.

The functional gas filler cap served as an ideal place to place an identifying badge, letting drivers in the 1967 Mustang's wake know what flew by.

Above: Brightwork was used to good effect in 1967, as seen on the fender badging on a 1967 Mustang hardtop.

Right: By 1967, the Mustang could be ordered with an increasing number of comfort and convenience options, including a tilt-away steering wheel and a reverb control mounted underneath the glove box.

The Mustang gained a bit of weight in 1967, yet retained the lithe lines of the first generation. Ford had big things planned for the Mustang, such as bigger engines, and that required room under the long hood. With the enlargement of the engine compartment, the rest of the vehicle grew to maintain its proportions. A base hardtop went for $2,461.46.

Price (base hardtop): $2,461.46

Engine: 289-ci, 225-horsepower, A-code V-8

Transmission: 4-speed manual

Total GT production: 24,079

Because the Kreidler and Krupp companies in West Germany already used the Mustang name to market small motorbikes and trucks, Ford was forced to market its über-auto the T-5. Due to a Ford company policy, it would not spend the $10,000 to buy the Mustang name. All T-5s were fitted with the heavy-duty suspension.

Price (base fastback): DM4,403 ($2,712)

Engine: 289-ci, 225-horsepower, A-code V-8

Transmission: 3-speed automatic,

Total T5 fastback production: 109

Left: On T-5s bound for West Germany, Ford installed a T-5 badge on the glove box door to replace the Mustang emblem found on American cars. Yet the horse emblem in the grille stayed put.

Below: Under the hood of the 1967, it was standard Mustang, no bad thing. The underhood export brace was installed on all T-5s.

Below: When the German auto press first drove the T-5, they were disappointed with the suspension on European roads, but Ford assured them that future T-5s would handle Continental driving with confidence. The Germans loved the powerful V-8 engine, though.

Rectangular driving lights were standard on 1968 Shelbys, and the "Green Hornet" was packed with every option imaginable. The huge grille opening allowed plenty of air to cool the huge 428-ci V-8.

Ten-spoke cast aluminum wheels were mated with Goodyear Polyglas tires in an attempt to restrain the 428-ci Cobra Jet engine.

Since the Mustang's earliest days, independent rear suspension was considered. Shelby installed a system underneath the EXP 500 within the existing space. Beefy tubular arms ensured durability.

Built as an engineering exercise, the 1968 Shelby EXP 500 tested the feasibility of Conelec fuel injection and independent rear suspension. Shelby project engineer Fred Goodell had the clout to hang onto it after it had been evaluated, saving it from the crusher, the normal fate for evaluation vehicles. The rare Shelby was called the "Green Hornet" due to its wild paint, and would be the only Shelby built with a vinyl roof.

Price: Experimental evaluation vehicle, not for public sale

Engine: 428-ci, Cobra Jet, 335-horsepower, R-code V-8

Transmission: 3-speed automatic

Total production: 1

A production run of 42,325 fastback Mustangs were built for the 1968 model year. For comparison, however, 249,447 hardtops rolled out of showrooms that year.

Like most American vehicles in the 1960s, the interior trim was styled with looks in mind, not safety. But it did make for a handsome cockpit.

Balchowski installed Koni shock absorbers and beefy springs, as well as fitting inner fender braces, to allow the stunt vehicles to withstand the rigor of stunt work.

Ford reaped incalculable publicity from the release of the 1968 Steve McQueen film *Bullitt*. The highlight of the movie was a vehicle chase through San Francisco with McQueen driving a 1968 Mustang 390 GT fastback and the villains using a 1968 Dodge 440 Charger R/T. Two Mustangs were prepared for the movie by Max Balchowski. The primary movie car was crushed after filming due to excessive damage incurred during its stunts. The backup car is rumored to be in Ohio where the owner has no intention of selling it.

Price: Motion picture stunt car, not for sale to the public

Engine: 390-ci, 325-horsepower, S-code V-8

Transmission: 4-speed manual

Total production: 2

Right: Modified for street competition, this 1968 Cobra Jet uses twin four-barrel carburetors to handle induction chores. The hood scoop covered the simple hole cut into the hood to allow cooler outside air to reach the engine compartment.

Below: Essentially a stock 1968 Mustang interior, the Cobra Jet's reason for being was to rack up mileage on the odometer a quarter-mile at a time.

Cobra Jets with four-speed manual transmissions used staggered rear shocks to help control rear-axle hop under hard acceleration. All of the first fifty Cobra Jets were fastback models.

In the latter half of 1968, Ford released the powerful 428-ci Cobra Jet engine in a run of 50 consecutive VIN Mustangs. They were painted white and went to "friends" of Ford that actively campaigned on the quarter-mile drag strips. Transmission options for the 428 Cobra Jet included a four-speed manual or a three-speed manual. *Hot Rod* magazine coaxed one down the drag strip in 13.56 seconds at 106.64 miles per hour.

Price (base fastback): $2,689.26, Cobra Jet option: $434

Engine: 428-ci, 335-horsepower, R-code V-8

Transmission: 4-speed manual

Total production: 50 (consecutive VINs)

Price (base hardtop): $2,578.60

Engine: 302-ci, 230-horsepower, J-code V-8

Transmission: 3-speed automatic

Total HCS production: 251

From 1966 through 1968, Colorado Ford dealers sold a High Country Special package for the Mustang. Denver Ford dealers advertised the High Country Special as "The most exciting Mustang since Mustang." It was available in any color or engine offering in the standard Mustang catalog. Production of the HCS model came to 251 units.

Above: The contrasting tape stripe on the rear of the spoiler was part of the HCS package.

Left: Located on the nonfunctional side scoop, the emblem for the High Country Special package was identical to the previous year's HCS, except the year on the emblem was updated.

For 1968, many of the styling cues from the GT/CS were incorporated. The vents on the hood were nonfunctional, but housed turn-signal indicators.

There were plenty of Shelby dress-up parts for the Mustang in 1968, and this California Special made full use of the catalog. Under the long Shelby air cleaner, twin carbs sit atop a 302-ci V-8.

The nonfunctional side scoops on the 1968 California Special were lifted directly from the Shelby parts bin. Tape graphics set them apart from the products of the man from Texas.

Unlike the exterior, the interior of the 1968 California Special was pure stock Mustang. The padded steering wheel was a concession to new federally mandated safety measures.

Conceived in Southern California, the GT/CS was a popular eye catcher. Both GT and non-GT Mustangs could be ordered with the GT/CS option, but GT wheel covers were placed on genuine GTs only. California Special script was on each rear quarter-panel, in case the rest of the package didn't tip people off. Federal regulations requiring side marker lights went into effect in 1968.

Price (base hardtop): $2,578.60

Engine: 302-ci, 230-horsepower, J-code V-8

Transmission: 3-speed automatic

Total CS production: 4,118

Right: The engine call-out on the Shaker Hood let the world know what was lurking underneath the expansive hood.

Below: Rear seat headroom was sacrificed for design. While the Mach 1 was considered a four-passenger vehicle, in the real world it was a 2+2.

As the engine displacements increased, so did the size of the Mustang. Faux scoops under the rear quarter windows were Shelby-like touch, except Shelby didn't use a scoop unless it was functional. Graceful SportsRoof proportions exuded muscle, which was exactly what Ford wanted to do in the midst of the muscle car wars. Quad headlights were a 1969-only design element.

Price (base SportsRoof): $2,618.00

Engine: 428-ci, 335-horsepower, Q-code V-8

Transmission: 4-speed manual

Total productions: 72,458

Price (base SportsRoof): $2,618.00

Engine: 428-ci, 335-horsepower, R-code V-8

Transmission: 4-speed manual

Total production: 312

One of the greatest deals in muscle cardom, the $6.53 3.91:1 Traction-Lok or 4.30:1 Detroit Locker rear axle ratio option in fact loaded the engine with serious go-fast parts. Using Ford GT MkIV LeMans 427-ci connecting rods, special forged aluminum pistons, and an external counter-balancer, this beast was destined to lord over the drag strip.

Mach 1s equipped with the Super Cobra Jet option used an oil cooler mounted ahead of the radiator support. On vehicles equipped with a Shaker hood scoop, a rubber skirt fit against the inside of the hood around the hole cut out for the scoop.

Above: The 1969 Mach 1 was the first muscle car to sport a Shaker hood scoop, which bolted directly to the air cleaner assembly. As the engine was revved, the scoop moved as the engine rocked on its mounts.

Left: Mustangs have had a side scoop since its introduction, and the 1969 Mach 1 was no exception. Like other years, it was non-functional, but contributed to the muscle car's menacing presence.

Price (above base SportsRoof): $1,208.35

Engine: 429-ci, 375-horsepower, Z-code V-8

Transmission: 4-speed manual

Total production: 869

Ford wanted to compete in the high profile NASCAR series, and in order to race its big 429-ci engine, the crescent-head motor had to be offered in a street car. The Mustang needed some modifications, such as hammering shock towers, to accept the huge powerplant, but the understated Boss 429 was disappointing until buyers fitted large carburetors and a set of headers. Then it was a 500-plus-horsepower monster, perfect for midnight milk runs.

Left: The hood scoop on the boss 429 was opened and shut via cable to a knob under the dash that the driver could operate at will. The 1969 Boss 429 hood scoops were painted with body color.

Below: Early 1969 Boss 429 production used "S" code engines filled with NASCAR-grade connecting rods and Cobra Jet hydraulic camshafts. They were toped with magnesium valve covers but changed to cast aluminum with the 280th Boss 429 built.

Discrete Boss 429 badging on the front fenders was the only obvious sign that the engine under the hood wasn't a pushover.

Right: The 290-horsepower small block featured large heads with massive valve ports, four-bolt main bearing caps, aluminum windage tray, forged steel connecting rods and crankshaft, forged aluminum pistons and a huge 780-cfm Holley carburetor. With 4.3:1 Detroit Locker rear end, the Boss could vault to 60 miles per hour in 5.5 seconds.

Below: A road race car with a license plate, designer Larry Shinoda insisted that the 1969 Boss 302 be built without a scoop beneath the rear quarter window.

Ford president Semon "Bunkie" Knudsen decreed that the Boss 302 should be "the best-handling street car available on the American market!" The result was pretty much spot on, as the race-honed suspension and high-revving engine made is a potent force in the SCCA's Trans-AM racing series and on the street. Famed designer Larry Shinoda styled the attention-grabbing graphic tape package. Only 1,628 were built in 1969.

> Price (above base SportsRoof): $676.15
>
> Engine: 302-ci, 290-horsepower, G-code V-8
>
> Transmission: 4-speed manual
>
> Total production: 1,628

The rear spoiler was adjustable for angle of attack. Due to Kansas City's propensity for tornadoes, it was felt that the label for the limited edition Mach 1s should reflect the area's high velocity heritage.

Cubic-inch call-outs that flank the Shaker Hood scoop left little doubt that the engine compartment was stuffed with good parts. Chrysler copied the exposed hood scoop starting in 1970 on their E-body models.

In 1970, the Mustang returned to a two-lamp headlight set-up. Inboard lights were turn signals.

The Kansas City Ford sales district was looking for a promotional Mustang, and Ford had a number of modified vehicles collecting dust after a supplier company went bankrupt. The result was the Twister Special, of which only 96 were built. The initial order for the Twisters was to be all 42 super Cobra Jets, but there weren't enough of the monster engines to go around and a number of 351 Clevelands were shipped in instead.

Price: $4,253.95

Engine: 428-ci, 335-horsepower, R-code

Transmission: 3-speed automatic

Total production: 96

Ford stylists worked with the Shelby staff to create a vehicle significantly different from its Mustang cousin.

Front fender scoops were intended to feed cooling air to the front disc brakes. How effective they were is a matter of conjecture.

The full-width grille housed a pair of headlights and the requisite Shelby logo. Lucas driving lamps kicked out 70,000 candlepower.

When the 1969 Mustang debuted, it had grown in almost every dimension, so it was inevitable that the Shelby version should follow suit. In fact, the Shelby GT350 and 500 were even longer than the Mustang, thanks to 21 separate pieces of plastic and fiberglass. A full-width grille opening fed air to the radiator, while five NACA ducts on the hood fed air in and out of the engine compartment, as well as the air cleaner. While it was essentially a gussied-up Mustang, it had Shelby's influence and name, and that counted for a lot.

No longer built for competing on tight race-tracks, the 1969 Shelbys were more at home on the open road—the straighter the better.

Price: $4,434

Engine: 351-ci, 290-horsepower, M-code V-8

Transmission: 3-speed automatic

Total 1969 Shelby production: 2,361

1970 SHELBY GT500

Price: $4,709

Engine: 428-ci, 335-horsepower, M-code V-8

Transmission: 4-speed manual

Total 1970 Shelby production: 789

By July 1969, there were still 1969-model Shelby vehicles sitting on dealer lots, so the unsold units were returned to Ford for modifications to be released as 1970 cars. Shelby himself saw that performance cars were waning, so he pulled the plug on the road cars. Under the supervision of an FBI agent, the dash mounted 1969 VIN tags were removed and replaced with 1970 tags. Some minor external changes were incorporated and the "new" cars were sent to dealers.

The 4-inch extension to the front of the 1970 Shelby GT500 is apparent from this perspective. Packing could be a challenge.

Twin stripes on the hood were the only external difference between 1969 and 1970 Shelbys.

The 428 Cobra Jet engine was a tight squeeze in the 1970 GT500. A 0–60-mile-per-hour time of 6.0 seconds was admirable, especially for a 3,850-pound vehicle.

Side stripes were offered in four colors: white, blue, black, and gold. The color of the stripe depended on which of the dozen body hues a buyer chose.

The 1970 Mach 1's base engine was this 351–ci Cleveland V-8, equipped with a two-barrel carburetor. Rated at 250 horsepower at 4,600 rpm, it made sufficient power to satisfy the Mach 1 buyers who wanted to look like they could blow someone's doors off even if the engine wasn't top-of-the-line.

The Mach 1 carried the performance banner for the Mustang starting in 1969, and continued into the mid 1970s. Its heritage was brought forward with the introduction of the Mach 1 Mustang in 2002.

Two transmissions were offered in the 1970 Mach 1: a three-speed automatic and a four-speed manual. Either one was effective at transmitting the engine's rotational energy into black lines on the pavement.

Stylistic changes in the 1970 Mach 1 included eliminating the scoops behind the door handles, returning to a two-lamp headlight system, and rocker panel treatment. The powerful 300-horsepower Cleveland engine debuted in the 1970 Mustang, costing only $48 in the Mach 1 and $93 in other Mustangs. Rear window Sport Slats were a $65 option, and the rear spoiler went for $20—it was only available on SportsRoof models.

Price (above base SportsRoof): $45.00

Engine: 351-ci, 250-horsepower, H-code V-8

Transmission: 3-speed automatic

Total production: 40,970

1971-1973

Chapter 3

A vicious circle. The Mustang that debuted for the 1971 model year was trapped in one. In order to maintain horsepower levels in the Mustang, a bigger engine was needed. To support a bigger engine, the suspension needed to be strengthened, and the body structure had to be enlarged. With the additional mass, a bigger engine was needed to propel the car. And with a bigger engine….

Two factors are key to understanding the physical growth of the Mustang for 1971. When the massive Boss 429 was fitted to the Mustang's engine compartment, Kar Kraft had to use hammers to make room. Ford executives felt that this was not the right way to build high performance vehicles, thus they decreed that the next generation of Mustang must be able to comfortably swallow any and all engines in the Ford roster.

The second part of the size equation was the recently introduced government regulations dictating the level of allowable emissions. Electronic engine management systems were in their infancy, so the auto manufacturer's had to resort to crude air pumps and retarded timing in an effort to meet the new standards. The inevitable loss of performance forced the auto makers to compensate for the restrictive smog equipment by increasing the displacement of the engines to maintain power levels. Thus the engines grew in size without an increase in grunt.

This isn't to say that the Mustang's 1971 lineup didn't have guts. The Boss 351 succeeded the Boss 302 in a bid for more Trans Am victories. Equipped with a more powerful 351-ci Cleveland V-8 developed for NASCAR competition, it was an easier engine to live with on the street, and it benefited from the hop-up tricks that Ford engineers had learned in the last few years. The suspension was tuned for better transitional response, and the brakes were improved. The result was one of the finest handling Mustangs ever built. Unfortunately, the day before the Detroit auto show where the world would be introduced to the Boss 351, Ford announced that it was stepping way from all forms of motorsports. This effectively shut the Boss 351 out of the Trans Am series, leaving it a race car in search of a race. It came as no surprise when the Boss 351 became a one-year vehicle.

For buyers desiring big-block thrills, one only had to check the "Cobra Jet" boxes. A change in engine families (385 engine series) resulted in the 429-ci V-8. While the block was based on the 460-ci engine, the heads had their roots in the free-breathing Cleveland design. Cobra Jet engines were built for rapid acceleration applications, and customers wanting the maximum amount of acceleration opted for the Drag Pak option, turning the Cobra Jet engine into a Super Cobra Jet. Functional Ram Air was available with the Cobra Jet options, as well as the Boss 351.

Back for another year was the Mach 1, sporting full-length body side stripes, and able to contain any V-8 in the Mustang menu with the exception of the 351 HO powerplant found in the Boss 351. Its base 302-ci engine generated 210-horsepower, while the 375-horsepower, 429-ci Super Cobra Jet was found at the top of the heap. Because the Mach 1 could be tailored from mild to wild, it had wider buyer appeal, resulting in impressive sales.

When the 1972 Mustang lineup was unveiled, it was evident that reality had landed at Ford. Unleaded gasoline hit the market, and Ford was the first manufacturer to engineer the entire product line to use the latest gasoline. Unfortunately, the lower octane rating of the fuel, combined with the reduced compression ratios needed to effectively reduce emissions, meant that the upward trend on engine power had come to a rapid halt. In fact, for 1972, all the big-block engines were deemed unsuitable in the Mustang.

The end of a full-sized Mustang was evident with the introduction of the 1973 line. Tape graphics and front 5-mile-per-hour bumpers were the biggest changes this year, as Ford was marking time until the all-new Mustang II hit the scene. The Cobra Jet engine option was still on the order sheet, still full of race-bred components, just toned down for the times. The Ford Maverick now filled the spot that the Mustang of 1965 had held in the lineup, that of a right-sized, sporty, affordable car, able to be tailored to the customer's needs and wants. The Mustang had grown into a Grand Touring vehicle, fit for huge engines and rapid acceleration. Breaking down the option preferences of buyers showed a leaning toward comfort and convenience, as 90.4 percent of 1973 Mustangs came with automatic transmissions, while 56.2 percent were equipped with air conditioning. However, while the Mustang was ensconced in the past, the future was running right past it.

Yet Mach 1 sales in 1973 far surpassed the prior year, as many performance enthusiasts realized that the end of an era was at hand, and it was either get one now or else.

The 1971 Mustang took a page from the Shelby design book with the adoption of a full-width grille, which tended to emphasize the two-inch increase in girth. Federal regulation decreed that 5-miles per hour bumpers grace the front of all new automobiles; on the Mustang, they added four inches to the overall vehicle length. Vertical turn signals and a body color front bumper cover were the only exterior changes from the preceding year.

Convertible Mustangs bid adieu in 1973 and stepped away from the market for a number of years. Forged aluminum wheels that debuted in 1973 had a flaw that forced Ford to recall them. *Photos courtesy of Mike Mueller*

Price: $3,189

Engine: 351-ci, 177-horsepower, H-code V-8

Transmission: 3-speed automatic

Total convertible production: 11,853

Even though the 1973 Mustang had been enlarged, the rear seats were still strictly 2+2.

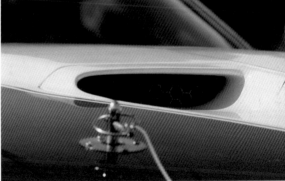

Hood pins lent a performance touch to the Mustang, as did the two-tone paint, which cost $34 on non–Mach 1 Mustangs.

Maintaining a Mustang tradition, tri-element taillights graced the stern of the 1973 Mustang.

Ford wanted to install the torque-heavy 429-ci engine into the Mustang, but its large dimensions necessitated a huge engine compartment. In that direction, the Mustang grew to fit the 385 Series motor. While the cast-iron block was based on the 460-ci engine, the heads used design architecture from the 351 Cleveland. The robust engine incorporated 4-bolt main bearing caps, 11.3:1 compression, and huge 2.25-inch intake valves to generate a tire-melting 450 lb-ft of torque. The quarter-mile strip could be covered in just 14.7 seconds at 96.2 miles per hour. Due to governmental regulations, this engine was available in the Mustang only in 1971, signaling the end of big-block engines in the original Pony Car.

Longer, lower, wider, the 1971 Mustang 429 Cobra Jet looked like it was moving even when it was standing still. *Photos courtesy of Mike Mueller*

Price, Mach 1 Mustang: $3,268

Engine: 429-ci, 370-horsepower, C-code V-8

Transmission: 4-speed manual

Total 429 CJ/SCJ production: 1,865

Under the large air cleaner lived a 4-barrel Quadrajet carburetor. The 429 Cobra Jet was a $372 option above the price of a base V-8.

Two transmissions were available with the 429 CJ engine, a close-ratio four-speed manual and a 3-speed C-6 Cruise-O-Matic automatic.

Filling the engine bay, the huge 429-ci engine was essentially a de-stroked 460-ci block. Aluminum valve covers were standard.

Price: $4,124

Engine: 351-ci, 339-horsepower, R-code V-8

Transmission: 4-speed manual

Total Boss 351 production: 1,806

Built for a race series that evaporated, the single-year Boss 351 had it all—a strong engine, taut competition suspension, and swoopy looks. Due to a corporate edict that the Mustang must be able to use any engine in the Ford roster, the engine compartment was huge. A one-inch increase in the wheelbase took it to 109 inches, while the overall length grew two inches. More metal meant more weight; the Boss 351 tipped the scales 600 pounds heavier than its predecessor.

Only 1,806 Boss 351s were built for 1971, the vehicles only year of manufacture.

The Boss 351 essentially used a stroked Boss 302 engine, including huge valves, a solid-lifter cam, and four-bolt main bearing caps.

Functional Ram Air hood scoops and locking pins were standard in the 1971 Boss 351. Two scoops fed a common plenum that sat on top of the air cleaner assembly.

With its Wünibald Kamm–inspired rear end designed to minimize drag, aerodynamics were starting to shape production vehicles.

The full range of Mustang models grew with the new 1971 design, including the Mach 1. Available with any V-8 in the catalog, the Mach 1 could range from mild, with a 210-horsepower 302-ci V-8, to wild, courtesy of a 375-horsepower 429-ci V-8. The biggest engine became a Super Cobra Jet with the fitting of the Drag Pack option, $155 well spent. Unfortunately, federal regulations on the horizon spelled the end of high-compression engines.

Classic pony car proportions were carried to extremes with the release of the 1971 Mach 1.

Price: $3,268

Engine: 351-ci, 285-horsepower, M-code V-8

Transmission: 3-speed automatic

Total Mach 1 production: 36,499

With a rear window only 14 degrees from horizontal, the 1971 Mustang Mach 1 sacrificed rear seat headroom for an aggressive profile.

The gas cap on the 1971 Mach 1 was a pop-open type, but in 1972 new emission regulations required a closed fuel system, dictating the use of a twist cap.

The crew at *Sports Car Graphic* magazine ran a 1971 Cobra Jet Mach 1 down the drag strip, reaching 60 miles per hour in 6.3 seconds, with a quarter-mile performance of 14.6 seconds at 99.4 miles per hour.

Essentially a carryover from 1971, the primary differences between the Mach 1 of 1971 and 1972 was what wasn't available. Under the hood, it was strictly small-block territory. Federal regulations had caught up with the high-horsepower engines, and rather than try to get the small production Boss 351 and 429 CJ engines cleaned up to pass emission tests, Ford pulled the plug. A low-compression version of the Boss 351 appeared as the 351 HO late in the model year, but production of this potent 275-horsepower V-8 was limited to only 398 units.

There were virtually no external differences for the 1972 Mach 1 from the year before, but under the long hood were small-block engines only. *Photos courtesy of Mike Mueller*

Price, Mach 1: $3,003

Engine: 351-ci, 266-horsepower, Q-code V-8

Transmission: 3-speed automatic

Production: 27,675

Like the year before, a full-length side stripe made a strong visual statement on the flanks of the 1972 Mach 1.

A wide range of engines was available in the Mach 1, from the base 302-ci V-8 to the 351-ci Cobra Jet.

Functional Ram Air induction was a $58 option with any 351-ci V-8.

Red pinstriping surrounded the blue panel between the taillights on the Sprint Décor optioned vehicles, a reference to the United States' involvement in the 1972 Olympics.

Two-tone seats were part of the Sprint Décor dress-up package, while the blue dash and carpets carried the color scheme through the entire interior.

There was no mistaking the country of origin of the Mustang Sprint.

Ford was not immune to Olympic spirit in 1972 when it released the Sprint Décor option for the Mustang, Maverick, and Pinto Runabout. The option consisted of white paint with blue rocker panels, stripes on the hood, a blue taillight panel, and special decals. The interior received a two-tone treatment. Any engine was available with the Sprint option, as well as any optional equipment that did not compromise the unique paint scheme. Fifty convertibles were built to participate in the 1972 Cherry Blossom Parade in Washington D. C.

The front bumper of the 1972 Mustang Sprint used a color-keyed front bumper to accentuate the vehicle's long lines. *Photos courtesy of Mike Mueller*

> Price, **Sprint Décor option**: $132.71
>
> **Engine**: 351-ci, 266-ci, Q-code V-8
>
> **Transmission**: 3-speed automatic
>
> **Production**: 9,383

Most 1973 Mustangs were equipped with wheel covers to save money. Forged aluminum wheels were a $118.77 option on the Grande model.

Cutting-edge automotive sound systems incorporated the 8-track tape player for the ultimate in sonic convenience.

Only four engines were offered, from a 1-barrel 250-ci six to a 4-barrel 351-ci V-8.

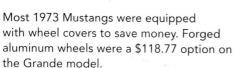

As the second generation of Mustangs came to an end, the 1973 model was little changed from the prior year. A slight front restyle and a change in tape graphics were the most evident differences. Federal regulations required 5-mile-per-hour front bumpers, and the color-keyed units on the Mustang were well integrated. Sales were down. In fact, the Maverick, similar in principle to the original Mustang, outsold its larger cousin. This was also the last year for the convertible model for quite some time.

For 1973, the front turn signals became vertical units, and the headlights were encircled in chrome. *Photos courtesy of Mike Mueller*

Price: $3,189

Engine: 351-ci, 177-horsepower, H-code V-8

Transmission: 3-speed automatic

Production: 11,853

Price: $3,088

Engine: 351-ci, 177-horsepower, H-code V-8

Transmission: 3-speed automatic

Total Mach 1 production: 35,440

It was soon common knowledge that the full-sized Mustang was going to be replaced in 1974 with a smaller, weaker rendition, so the fence-sitters wanting a classic Mach 1 stepped forward in impressive numbers. Ford engineers worked hard to retain some performance in the car in the face of increasingly stringent federal emission regulations. Unleaded gasoline was now washing across the land, and with it, tire-shredding performance fell by the wayside.

In 1973, the Mach 1 used a 140-horsepower, 302-ci engine as the base unit. Two 351-ci V-8s were optional; the top-shelf Cobra Jet delivered 266 horsepower.

For 1973, the Mach 1 sported different side-stripe treatment with the logo in front of the rear wheels. As in years before, the tape stripe was reflective.

Sales for the 1973 Mach 1 increased from the year before to 35,440. The prior year saw 27,675 units sold.

As comfort was an increasingly demanded commodity in performance cars, 90.4 percent of 1973 Mustangs came with automatic transmissions, while 56.2 percent enjoyed air conditioning.

Performance enthusiasts within Ford worked hard to keep the muscle in the 1973 Mustang, even to the point of bending the EPA regulations. The subdued 351-ci two-barrel engine emissions data was used to try to certify potent four-barrel Q-code Cobra Jet Ram Air for use in the Mach 1. The government caught Ford at this ploy, and forced it to use the lower rated engine in the Mach 1. It was not possible to get functional Ram Air with the Cobra Jet engine.

A sleeper in Mustang clothes, this 1973 coupe was the hot car for the year, thanks to a Cobra Jet engine.

Price: $2,847

Engine: 351-ci, 266-horsepower, Q-code V-8

Transmission: 3-speed automatic

Total Coupe production: 51,480

Luxury, 1973 Mustang–style. The Tilt-Away steering wheel, a $41 option, was handy for the long-legged driver, while the $204 Select Shift Cruise-O-Matic automatic transmission was installed in more that 90 percent of 1973 Mustangs.

While the vertical rear taillight panel helped the aerodynamics, the airflow tended to soil the back of the vehicle, including the tri-element taillights.

Buyers had to pony up $194 for the 266-horsepower Cobra Jet engine.

1974-1978

Chapter 4

At the annual stockholders meeting in 1968, Ford executives faced a shareholder demanding that the Mustang be kept small and nimble. Henry Ford II, known behind his back as "The Deuce," took note and started the wheels turning toward the project that would become the Mustang II. He authorized the construction of two mock-ups: a Pinto-based vehicle codenamed Arizona, and a Maverick-based car called Ohio. Extensive market research concluded that Arizona would be more likely to succeed in the showroom.

Lee Iacocca insisted that the new Mustang II be small, and to that end decreed that a straight-six cylinder engine, long a staple in the Mustang, be set aside due to its length. Instead, a German-built V-6 was pressed into duty, along with a base inline four cylinder engine. A bigger problem lay in the design of the new car. Iacocca didn't like any of the 50 clay models that were created. Finally, design chief Al Mueller's staff put together a car that used many styling cues from the 1965 Mustang, and Iacocca signed off on it.

Buyers wanting a vehicle with a sporty flavor tended to lean towards the Mach 1, packing the 2.8-liter V-6 as standard. Its 105-horsepower didn't set the world on fire, but any vehicle tipping the scales at almost 3,000 pounds with that kind of power would have behaved in a similarly languid fashion. Visually, the Mach 1 looked like a mini-muscle car, but the response when the accelerator was slammed down was disappointing to drivers weaned on Boss 429s and K-codes.

Fortunately for the Ford Motor Company, the vast majority of buyers couldn't have cared less about the Mustang II's inability to shred a set of tires at a stop light. Gasoline prices were starting a serious climb, and suddenly driving a vehicle that got 10 miles per gallon on a good day didn't make sense. Ford had the right vehicle at the right time, and with 385,993 sold in 1974, the champagne was flowing in Dearborn. *Motor Trend* magazine gave the Mustang II its prestigious Car of the Year award, confirming The Deuce's and Iacocca's decision to push for a small car.

Performance, in the form of a 302-ci V-8 mated to an automatic transmission, returned to the Mustang in 1975, its 140 horsepower much appreciated by enthusiasts. At the opposite end of the engine spectrum, Ford offered an MPG edition, mating the 88-horsepower, 2.3-liter inline four cylinder engine with a 3.18:1 rear axle ratio. A healthy kid on a ten-speed could beat it off the line. Sales for the 1975 Mustang II were about half of the prior year, yet 187,567 vehicles sold is an impressive number.

Ford introduced a storied name from years past when it unveiled the Mustang II Cobra II in 1976. Splashy graphics and black-out paint made for an eye-catching package, and while any size engine could be ordered in the Cobra II, the 302-ci V-8 and four-speed manual transmission were the closest thing to old-school performance. Ford engineers had tweaked the suspension bits, resulting in crisper handling. The Cobra II conversion was done by a company called Motortown, owned by famed public relations whiz Jim Wangers, responsible for the Pontiac GTO. Some of the Cobra II sales literature even featured Carroll Shelby.

In an effort to control costs, the Cobra II modifications were brought in-house. While the choices of engines were merely three, the option sheet was as long as a buyer's arm, offering everything but the kitchen sink. Mach 1 sales were slowly slipping each year, yet a sufficient number were sold to retain the model.

As the Mustang II entered its last year of production, Ford pulled out all the stops, offering a King Cobra option, priced at a staggering $1,277! To put things into perspective, the 1970 Boss 429 option cost $1,208. For the long green, a King Cobra buyer got the Cobra II's hood scoop and rear spoiler, cross-lace alloy wheels, a special air dam/splitter, and unique tape graphics. Under the hood, it was the standard 139-horsepower, 302-ci V-8. Now that's value!

This was also the year that the government's Corporate Average Fuel Economy (CAFE) started, and it would go a long way in determining a manufacturer's product mix. For every vehicle that got no better than 17 miles per gallon, the auto maker would need to build a car that got better than 19 miles per gallon, the average being 18 miles per gallon.

While some people mock the Mustang II as a slow, ungainly shadow of the original Mustang, it can't be denied that the Mustang II kept the marque alive. Chrysler pulled the plug on the Barracuda and Challenger at the end of 1974, while GM's Camaro and Firebird limped along with anemic offerings. If the Mustang II had not been the success it was, the Mustang line would have ended many years ago. We all have the Mustang II to thank for keeping the brand alive.

With the introduction of the Mustang II in 1974, Ford went backward to go forward. Like the original Mustang, the II used an economy car (Pinto) as a basis. When the Mustang II debuted, the only engines available were an inline four-cylinder and a German-sourced V-6. A V-8 returned to the menu in 1975. With an oil crisis in the mid-1970s, the Mustang II was the right car for the times.

Styling cues from the 1965 Mustang were evident, including the oval grille, single headlights, and side-mounted C-scoop. *Photos courtesy of Mike Mueller*

Price: $3,818

Engine: 140-ci, 2.3L, 88-horsepower, Y-code I-4

Transmission: 4-speed manual

Production, hatchback: 51,100

Thirteen-inch wheels were standard on the Mustang II. Wheel covers were meant to evoke first generation Mustangs.

The Mustang II was available in two body styles: notchback sedan and a three-door hatchback.

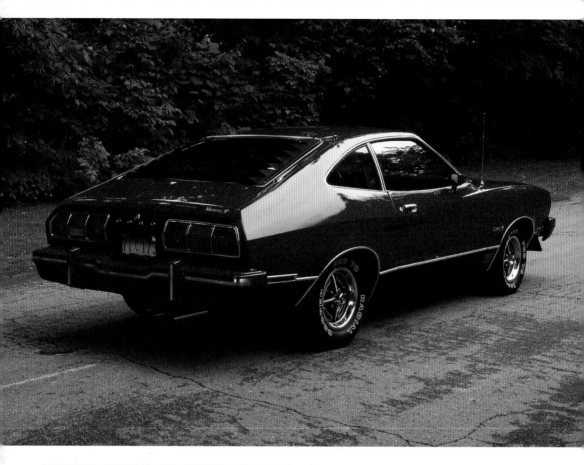

Price: $4,188

Engine: 302-ci, 5.0L, 140-horsepower,
    F-code V-8

Transmission: 3-speed SelectShift automatic

Production: 21,062

The V-8 engine returned to the Mustang stable in 1975, although it was a shadow of former days. While the vehicle was not designed for a V-8, Ford engineers shoehorned a 302-ci small-block into the diminutive engine compartment. Even though the engine used a two-barrel carburetor, mileage was abysmal, getting only 13.7 miles per gallon in the city, 15.9 on the highway. Top speed was about 105 miles per hour, and the drag strip required 17.9 seconds to conquer, with a trap speed of 77 miles per hour.

The grille was moved forward to a nearly flush design to allow the V-8 to fit under the hood. *Photos courtesy of Mike Mueller*

Tri-element lenses harkened back to early Mustangs, and kept this important styling cue alive.

Only one transmission was available with the V-8, the 3-speed SelectShift automatic.

Price, V-8 Hardtop: $3,737

Engine: 302-ci, 139-horsepower, F-code V-8

Transmission: 3-speed automatic

Total hatchback production: 62,312

Many auto enthusiasts moaned when Ford introduced the small Mustang II in 1974, yet it was *Motor Trend* magazine's Car of the Year, and sales went through the roof. Granted, real performance was a shadow of former years, but Ford massaged a small-block V-8 and used decals and badging to visually separate the Cobra II from the pack. The Cobra II package cost $325, while the Cobra modification package went for $287 and included front and rear spoilers, faux hood scoop, quarter-window louvers, and lots of stripes.

The Cobra II was available with any engine in the Mustang II lineup, from the 92-horsepower, 140-ci inline four to the 139-horsepower, 302-ci V-8.

Tri-element taillights continued to be used on the Mustang II platform. Large decals let people in the Cobra II's wake know they were in the presence of mid-Seventies performance.

The Mustang II Cobra II's wheelbase was only 96.2 inches, a full foot shorter that the original 1965 Mustang.

Price: $6,890

Engine: 302-ci, 134-horsepower, F-code V-8

Transmission: 3-speed automatic

Total King Cobra production: 4,318

Who would have thought that a few years after the mighty Boss 429 engine, an option package would rival it in price. The visually spectacular King Cobra option went for a hefty $1,277 and all of the changes were cosmetic. Beneath the skin, the standard 302-ci V-8 and related mechanicals did their job. On the drag strip, it could run the length in 16.59 seconds at 82.41 miles per hour. Not bad for a 3,300-pound vehicle breathing through a two-barrel carburetor.

Based on the Pinto platform, the reduced size of the Mustang II is evident in a side view.

A low-compression 302-ci V-8 lived under the King Cobra's hood, cranking out all of 134 horsepower, while fuel mileage hovered in the 13-miles per gallon range.

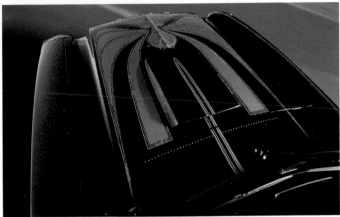

The three-door fastback had almost every gee-whiz styling touch imaginable, including a giant Cobra hood decal, fake hood scoop, and tape stripes, which were strategically placed on the rocker panels, rear deck and roof.

Tape stripes and rear window louvers were part of the $1,277 King Cobra option. A huge rear spoiler came in handy, as the top speed was almost 120 miles per hour.

With performance on the back burner, the Mustang II's engine didn't get much attention from the stylists.

Ford's long relationship with Ghia design in Italy has produced many memorable vehicles, including the 1978 Mustang II Ghia.

The blacked-out egg crate grille set off the chrome galloping pony on the 1978 Mustang II Ghia model. The lights in the grille were actually turn-signals.

When Lee Iacocca laid out the design philosophy for the Mustang II, he wanted a "little limousine." The Ghia was the closest the Mustang II got to his wishes. From its sumptuous interior to the partial vinyl roof, it spoke luxury. The full slate of available engines could be slipped into the Ghia model, from the 88-horsepower, 140-ci, inline four-cylinder to the 302-ci, 139-horsepower V-8. The Ghia Sports Group option cost $386.

Aerodynamics took a back seat to style on the Mustang II Ghia, as the bluff front end didn't quite cut the air cleanly. But the familial line of the 1965 model was unmistakable.

Price: $4,242

Engine: 302-ci, 139-horsepower, F-code, V-8

Transmission: 3-speed automatic

Total Ghia production: 34,730

1979-1993

Chapter 5

The next generation of Mustang was released in late 1978, but was born in late 1972. Hal Sperlich in product planning saw that a common platform could be used under a four-door sedan as well as a sporty car. It was code-named Fox. Much work was done on the Fox Mustang by engineering, but by 1974 the challenges of designing a car that would satisfy the myriad regulations in Europe as well as America proved to be insurmountable.

In the spring of 1975, Sperlich's Fox program was taken over by North American Automobile Operations (NAAO), and they quickly set dates for the introduction for the Fairmont sedan (1977) and the Mustang (1979). The final design came from Jack Telnack's team creating the "semi-fastback," sort of a modern version of the original fastback from 1965. Not only did it look good, it sliced through the air better than its predecessor, reducing drag six percent.

Under the hood, the 1979 Mustang was a scene of some change. Part way through the year, the V-6 engine was replaced with the old 200-ci straight-six mill. For the first time, a turbocharged engine was available, the 2.3-liter four-cylinder motor generating 132 horsepower. For lovers of V-8 power, the 5.0-liter was the strongest engine on the menu, dishing out all of 140 horsepower.

Little changed in Mustangland in 1980. Yet the basis for real performance was quietly being laid. In 1981, a 4-speed with overdrive manual transmission was introduced. Another performance aid was the availability of a Traction-Lok rear end, which went a long way to reducing axle hop and wheelspin under heavy acceleration. While the 4.2-liter engine couldn't generate much in the way of tire-shredding grunt, the downstream components were ready.

The performance scene changed in 1982 with the re-introduction of the 5.0-liter HO engine. Now it was rated at 157 horsepower (to compete with the Camaro and Firebird) and attractive to the California Highway Patrol. Another blast from the past that returned was the GT option, replete with non-functional hood scoop, front and rear spoilers and appropriate badging.

In 1983, the convertible Mustang returned to a public hungry for fun. With ragtop sales of 23,438 units, it was clear to Ford execs that this was one of their better ideas. Midway through the model year, the 2.3-liter turbocharged engine found in the Thunderbird was slipped into the Mustang, now making 145 horsepower. Only installed in GT hatchbacks, it wasn't the biggest seller at 556 units. It was cheaper to buy a GT with the 175-horsepower, 5.0-liter V-8, and with 27,995 sold, it was clear that this kind of math was popular with buyers.

The biggest news for 1984 was the mid-year introduction of the Special Vehicle Operations (SVO) Mustang. SVO was an in-house organization designed to create high-performance parts and vehicles, and their opening act was a 175-horsepower, 2.3-liter, 4-cylinder, intercooled, turbocharged vehicle that could find its way around a corner better than any prior Mustang. From its smooth front end to its distinctive bi-plane rear spoiler, it reeked unique. Not an inexpensive piece, some $6,000 more that a GT, it sold in relatively small numbers: 4,057.

The promise of more power was made good in 1985, when the 5.0-liter V-8 enjoyed a boost in horsepower. Now rated at 210, it was accomplished by the use of forged pistons,

a hydraulic roller lifter assembly, and a freer-breathing exhaust system. Another recipient of technology was the SVO model, which now cranked out 205 horsepower due to a hotter camshaft, split exhaust system, bigger fuel injection nozzles, and a score of other refinements. Pity the customers didn't appreciate all of that work, as only 1,951 were sold.

When 1986 came into view, SVO was heading out the door. With sales this year of 3,379 units, it was clear that more people were becoming aware of the seriousness of the package, but it was too little too late. On a positive note, the 5.0-liter V-8 now used sequential electronic multipoint fuel injection, which along with a true dual exhaust system, improved drivability. The return of performance was underway, and the benefits would become apparent over the next several model years.

Bigger news in 1993 was the debut of the Mustang Cobra built by the successor to SVO, Special Vehicle Team (SVT). Built to raise the performance level of the Mustang to new heights, it used a massaged 5.0-liter V-8 rated at 235 horsepower and a highly tuned suspension to create a stormer. For buyers wanting to compete in showroom stock racing, an "R" model was created. While the Cobra was not built in large numbers (5,100), it generated tremendous press for the entire Mustang line.

Ford had big plans for the Mustang in 1994, and the Fox platform as it was developed in the mid-1970s era was finally going to be put to rest. Yet the Mustang had prospered with the Fox architecture, and had grown from a sporty vehicle to a true sports car.

Reclining Recaro seats were installed in the Pace Car replicas, the first time a reclining seat was used in a Mustang.

An egg-crate grille was carried over from previous years, maintaining a visual thread with older Mustangs.

Having first debuted at the 500 in 1964, the Mustang's second pace car appearance at Indianapolis came for the 63rd running in 1979.

Officials at the Indianapolis Motor Speedway tapped the Mustang to pace the famous 500-mile race for 1979. The actual pace cars were prepped by Jack Roush to run much longer than a full 500 miles at 125 miles per hour. To commemorate the occasion, Ford released 11,000 Indy Pace Car replicas without Roush's modifications. While the Pace Car was only offered in a three-door hatchback configuration, the V-8 had its bore reduced in an effort to comply with corporate average fuel economy (CAFE) figures. The resulting 255-ci did little to boost performance.

The Indy Pace Car replicas and the Cobras were equipped with the top-of-the-line Special Suspension that incorporated Michelin's TRX low-profile tires and metric cast-aluminum wheels.

Price, standard hatchback: $4,828

Engine: 255-ci, 140-horsepower, F-code V-8

Transmission: 4-speed manual

Total Pace Car production: 10,478

The Fox-bodied Mustangs that debuted in 1979 were noted for their clean interior, with spare lines and easy-to-read instruments.

The SelectShift automatic transmission was a #307 option. Cigarette burns on the carpet are reputed to have been caused by actress Bette Davis.

A plastic grille with rectangular holes was a Ford styling cue used across virtually the entire Ford line.

The third generation of Mustangs debuted in 1979 and was built on the Fox unit-body platform, shared with the Ford Fairmont and Mercury Zephyr, in an attempt to amortize costs. The wheelbase grew 4.2 inches to 100.4, which enabled the interior to be enlarged and smoothed the ride. For the first time in Mustang history, the rear axle was located by a four-bar link setup and coil springs. This car, the last vehicle owned by actress Bette Davis, was purchased to allow her to travel unrecognized.

The trim 1980 Mustang sedan was basically a carryover from 1979. The 302-ci engine was downsized to 255-ci, as its power output fell to just 119 horsepower.

Price: $5,338

Engine: 2.3L, 90-horsepower, A-code Inline 4-cylinder

Transmission: 3-speed automatic

Total coupe production: 128,893

For the first time since 1973, a convertible Mustang graced the showroom floor. Ford was not sure that the public would buy a convertible Mustang, so they contracted out a ragtop conversion to Cars & Concepts of Brighton, Michigan. Notchbacks were delivered from the factory, and C&C transformed them into hair-tousled fun. Any engine could be ordered with the convertible except for the four-cylinder/automatic transmission combo.

More a 2+2 than a true four-seater, the convertible begged to have friends pile into the back seats and soak up the sun. *Photos courtesy of Mike Mueller*

Price: $6,369

Engine: 5.0L, 175-horsepower, F-code V-8

Transmission: 3-speed automatic

Production: 23,438

As the power output of the Mustang increased, so did tire size, now up to a 14-inch wheel.

Following the trend, Ford equipped the Mustang with a plethora of warning lights. They were cheaper than instruments.

The 1984 Mustang SVO was the first 'Stang that didn't have a "proper" grille. It was one of the first American cars that pulled the majority of its cooling air from under the front bumper.

Ford used discreet badging on the SVO. With the huge polycarbonate twin-deck spoiler and smooth front end, the vehicle didn't need splashy graphics.

From the mouse-hair dash panel to the short-throw shifter, the Mustang SVO's interior was designed for sport driving.

The Mustang came very close to becoming a front-wheel-drive vehicle in the early 1980s, as Mazda's MX-6 was tapped to be rebadged as a Mustang, saving Ford billions of dollars. Yet Ford wanted to raise its profile in the racing world, and Special Vehicle Operations chief Michael Kranefuss pushed for the use of the Mustang as a banner-carrying sporty street car. The resulting Mustang SVO became a performance legend the day it was released.

The SVO was designed to accommodate flush "aero" headlamps. Following its introduction in mid-1984 with standard sealed-beam headlights such as these, it was not until late June 1985 that models were able to take advantage of federal rules on headlight systems.

Price: $15,585

Engine: 2.3L, 175-horsepower, W-code, turbocharged inline 4-cylinder

Transmission: 5-speed manual

Total SVO production: 4,508

Price: $13,441

Engine: 2.3L, 145-horsepower, turbocharged inline-four

Transmission: 5-speed manual

Total Mustang GT350 convertible production: 104

To commemorate 20 years of model history, Ford released the 1984 Twentieth Anniversary Edition GT350. The only problem was that Ford thought they owned the rights to the GT350 name, when in fact Carroll Shelby did. When the vehicle was introduced, Shelby filed a lawsuit and won. Production of the GT350 Mustang was completed in 35 days of production, from March 5, 1984, to April 1984. Thus production was very low, and today they are very rare.

The GT350 received numerous suspension enhancements, such as a modified MacPherson strut front suspension with an antiroll bar, and a four-link rear axle with special coil springs and gas-filled shock absorbers.

Two engines were offered in the 1984 GT 350, a 175-horsepower, 5.0-liter High Output V-8 and a 145-horsepower, 2.3-liter turbocharged inline four-cylinder.

Special P220/55R390 Michelin TRX metric tires were mounted on the 1984 20th Anniversary Edition Turbo GT 350.

While the folded convertible stack did not slip completely from view, it did let the occupants hear the whine of the non-intercooled turbocharger in the Turbo GT 350's 2.3-liter, inline-four engine.

Price: $13,441

Engine: 2.3L, 145-horsepower, T-code, turbocharged inline 4-cylinder

Transmission: 5-speed manual

Total GT Turbo Convertible production: 104

Ford took advantage of the improved Mustang platform to introduce a number of models, including the swift GT Turbo. It used the same 2.3-liter engine as the SVO, except the output was reduced to 145 horsepower to avoid stepping on the SVO's toes. Confusion set in on the showroom, as the 5.0-liter V-8 was also offered and customers tended to buy the torque-heavy V-8 rather than the peaky turbo engine. As a result, sales were soft, and Ford pulled the plug on the model within two years.

While structural rigidity took a back seat to alfresco fun, the 1984 GT Turbo Convertible was a lifestyle automobile that could find its way around a corner.

The woefully inadequate speedometer in the GT Turbo could be put past the 85-miles-per-hour mark with relative ease. Crisp white-on-black instrumentation allowed for rapid reading of the dials at speed.

The cast-aluminum pieces found on the GT Turbo were essentially the same wheel that had been available since 1978. They were designed to use only metric-sized tires.

The hood scoop on the 1984 GT Turbo was for engine clearance and not for ingesting cool ambient air.

Price: $15,272

Engine: 2.3L, turbocharged, 200-horsepower, W-code Inline-4

Transmission: 5-speed manual

Production: 3,028

In what seemed to some as a step backwards, Special Vehicle Operations, Ford's Skunk Works, retained the turbocharged four-cylinder engine. While the powerplant generated controversy, the way the SVO went around a corner generated smiles. The biplane rear spoiler could be deleted and replaced with the unit from the GT. The power rating was lowered five horsepower for 1986 due to the use of lower octane fuel. This would be the SVO's last year of production.

Flush wheels, a smooth grille, and wind deflector spats in front of the rear tires were some of the aerodynamic tricks Ford stylists used to reduce wind drag. *Photos courtesy of Mike Mueller*

The SVO's dashboard was all business, with full instrumentation and a leather covered steering wheel and shifter.

The air-to-air intercooler mated with the functional scoop on the hood to reduce the temperature of the induction charge.

The 90-degree, 5.0-liter high-output engine cranked out 225 horsepower and 300 lb-ft of torque.

The 1987 Mustang GT 5.0-liter used lower body cladding extensively, including a faux front brake cooling scoop. The top speed was 148 miles per hour.

Louvered taillights were a stylistic touch that most people either loved or hated.
The functional bumpers were nicely integrated into the overall design.

The Mustang was growing muscles, and the public ate it up. Automotive electronics had gotten to the point where power and fuel mileage could be increased, while emissions were reduced. The V-8 engine was back in a big way, and even law enforcement used the potent pony car as a pursuit vehicle. The 5.0-liter Mustang could cover the quarter-mile in 15.5 seconds at 93.0 miles per hour. The V-8 could be fitted to any non-GT Mustang for only $1,885, a real performance bargain.

Tautly styled, well-engineered, aggressively priced, these were unbeatable ingredients that Ford combined to make the 1987 GT the top pony car of its day.

Price: $12,106

Engine: 5.0L, 225-horsepower, M-code V-8

Transmission: 5-speed manual

Total hatchback production: 94,441

Showing that there is no substitute for cubic inches, the venerable 5.0-liter V-8 continued to propel the Mustang to high sales. Improvements in electronic ignition systems led the way to increased power with lowered emissions and improved fuel economy. The public ate it up like free candy. Only two engines were available, a diminutive 88-horsepower inline 4-cylinder and the beefy 225-horsepower, 5.0-liter V-8. Enjoying power with the sun in your face was the ideal way to travel. Still is.

Lower sill extensions were unique to the GT model, and gave the vehicle a buff, broad-shouldered look. *Photos courtesy of Mike Mueller*

Price: $16,610

Engine: 5.0L, EFI 225-horsepower, E-code V-8

Transmission: 4-speed automatic

Production: 18,174

Tuned intake runners helped in providing good low- and mid-range power, while letting the engine breath deeply at high rpms.

A clean, squarish design dominated the interior, as the instrumentation was easily readable and the controls easy to reach.

Price: $36,500

Engine: 5.0L, 292-horsepower, V-8

Transmission: 5-speed manual

Total SSC production: 160

Former Mustang race car driver turned car builder Steve Saleen introduced his line of modified Mustangs in 1984, and by 1989 the SSC was taken seriously as a premium sport muscle car. More a race car with a license plate frame, the SSC had a race-honed suspension, serious driver's cockpit, and splashy exterior graphics. Each vehicle was numbered on the front bumper under the headlight, and each SSC was the answer to the questions "How fast do you want to go?" and "How much money do you want to spend?"

Steve Saleen built just 160 Saleen SSCs in 1989. Equipped with 16-inch wheels on a stiffened chassis and Monroe adjustable shock absorbers, this street fighter topped out at 156 miles per hour.

Left: Discretion behind the wheel is suggested with the high-profile stance of the 1989 Saleen SSC

Below: A Momo steering wheel was available for 1987 only. Cruise control buttons were a concession to real-world driving.

Saleen massaged the 1989 SSC engine with an enlarged throttle body, improved rocker arm ratios, ported and polished heads, and AirSensors TPO unit, and stainless steel headers.

As the last decade of the century began, there were few other vehicles that could deliver more bang for the buck as a Fox-platform 5.0-liter LX. Add the benefits of a convertible top, and life doesn't get much better. The rear luggage rack on the 1990 Mustang LX was not really meant to carry luggage, but it did provide a mounting position for the center-mount brake light. With a torque-happy V-8 under the hood, most people tended to see the rear of the Mustang LX 5.0, a lot.

Ordering the 5.0-liter LX the buyer received the same suspension and tires as the GT model without the ticket-baiting spoilers and air dam.

Price: $17,796

Engine: 5.0L, 225-horsepower, M-code V-8

Transmission: 5-speed manual

Total LX production: 44,851

To commemorate the 25th anniversary of the Mustang, Ford fitted a special badge to the passenger side of the dashboard.

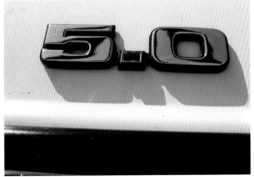

It didn't take much of a push against the gas pedal to make the 140-miles-per-hour speedometer needle jump to the north end of the scale. Great fun.

A welcome sign to lovers of Ford performance, the 5.0 badge on the side of the 1990 LX Mustang denoted a 5.0-liter engine the long hood. A favorite with the smoking-tire set, the small-block engine has proven remarkably durable.

Price: $26,921

Engine: 5.0L, EFI 225-horsepower, M-code V-8

Transmission: 4-speed automatic

Production: 65

In an attempt to widen the appeal of the Mustang, American Sunroof Corporation teamed with McLaren to build special versions of the Mustang. Introduced in 1984, it incorporated a lowered suspension, leather seats, special center console, top-shelf stereo system, and 15x7 McLaren wheels shod with Goodyear Gatorback tires. Exterior add-ons were kept to a minimum, resulting in a fleet, great-handling vehicle that didn't scream "look at me." Due to a disagreement between ASC and other parties, 1990 was the final year of manufacture.

Clean lines and tasteful body modifications were a signature ASC McLaren hallmark. *Photos courtesy of Mike Mueller*

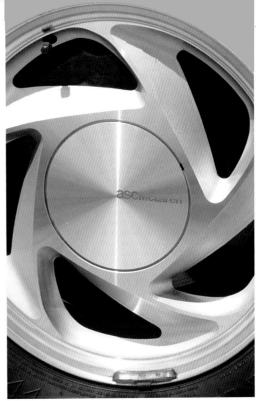

Special leather seating surfaces with ASC McLaren stitching helped set the interior apart form standard Mustangs.

Sticky P225/60VR15 Goodyear Gatorback radial tires worked with the 15x7 cast aluminum wheels and lowered suspension to keep the modified Mustang glued to the road.

On a twisty road, this was the view most drivers had of the ASC McLaren, as its tuned suspension allowed it to track like a slot car.

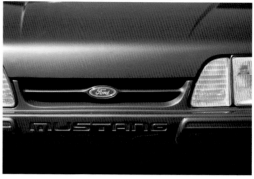

An aluminum intake helped hold weight down on the 5.0-liter V-8, as well as look sharp.

A minimalist grille and aero headlights helped the 1993 Mustang LX reduce the drag coefficient to 0.39

Since the first Mustang rolled off of the assembly line, the interior could best be described as a 2+2, and the 1993 version didn't break out of that mold.

Sales of the Mustang in the last year (1993) before a major restyle were excellent, and 114,228 rolled off showroom floors. Ford changed the method of rating engine output in 1993, which resulted in the 5.0-liter V-8 coming in at 205 horsepower, down 20 from the year before. In reality, it still had the same kick the pants grunt of the prior year. Dual exhaust was part of the 5.0-liter package, whether it was installed in an LX or a GT.

The Mustang would ride on the Fox platform for an astounding 15 years, testament to the soundness of the design.

Price: $15,150

Engine: 5.0L, 205-horsepower, E-code V-8

Transmission: 5-speed manual

Total LX 5.0L production: 22,902

1994-2004

Chapter 6

A small group within Ford Motor Company started the process of replacing the Fox-based Mustang in late 1998. Mustang engineering design manager John Colletti headed a Skunk Works organization that investigated the feasibility of making the next generation of Mustang substantially stiffer, fast, and sleeker.

In June 1990, Colletti's Skunk Works group was dissolved, replaced by "Team Mustang." Changes to the Fox-4 platform were dimensionally modest; the wheelbase was extended just 0.8 inch to 101.3 inches. Both front and rear tracks were widened 1.9 inches on the GT. Yet numbers didn't tell of the significant changes the platform enjoyed. Computer aided design allowed engineers to quickly test their work, so by the time the final platform design was set in stone, there was no area that had not been changed for the better.

Ford introduced the 1994 model Mustang on December 9, 1993, and it was clear that it

was a significant evolutionary step forward. Its interior was a dual-cowl design, much like the 1965 model. Flowing curves worked with classic Mustang styling cues to create a vehicle that was unmistakably Mustang. Changes under the hood were worth a closer look, as the 2.3-liter four-cylinder engine was pulled from the lineup. In its place as the base engine was the 3.8-liter V-6, last seen in the 1986 Mustang. In this incarnation, it used tuned port fuel injection and tubular headers to generate 145 horsepower. GT models used the 5.0-liter V-8, now rated at 215 ponies. The SVT Cobra was tweaked to pump out 240 horsepower, and was tapped to pace the Indianapolis 500.

While the 1995 Mustang was essentially a carry-over from the prior year, news was made at SVT. Reprising a model last seen in 1993, the "R" was equipped with a 5.8-liter V-8 generating 300 horsepower. Limited to just 250 units, buyers had to show their valid competition license to buy one. Within 10 hours of the vehicle going on sale, they had all been snapped up.

Big news in the Mustang world hit for model year 1996. The very long-running 5.0-liter V-8 was sent out to pasture, replaced by a 4.6-liter "modular" V-8. Instead of pushrods and rocker arms, the new engine used single overhead camshafts to activate the intake and exhaust valves. Even though the new engine displaced 31 cubic inches less than its predecessor, it delivered the same rated horsepower, 215. It's just that the engine had to be revved higher to extract the power.

When the Mustang for 1999 was unveiled, its crisp lines and aggressive stance were in sharp contrast to the "melted" look of prior years. The V-6 was fitted with a balance shaft, a new intake manifold and modified cylinder heads to raise its power to 190 horsepower. Even more power was available courtesy of the 4.6-liter V-8. By slipping in a new camshaft, bolting on an improved intake manifold, and fitting coil-on-plug ignition, 260 horsepower was extracted.

The 2000 model year saw virtually no change in the Mustang camp, but another one-year-only Cobra "R" hit the streets, brasher and brawnier than every before. Just 300 lucky buyers took home an IRS-equipped, side-exhaust, spoiler-equipped ground pounder. Devoid of air conditioning, radio, rear seat and sound suppression material, it was a 186-miles-per-hour street-legal race car.

For 2002, the biggest news was what wasn't available—the SVT Cobra. A one-year hiatus from the market allowed the small crew at SVT to prepare a seriously potent car for a 2003 release. And SVT wasn't the only group unveiling a head-turner in 2003, Team Mustang had been working overtime to bring a blast from the past back to life, with dramatic results.

First the Cobra. The SVT folks looked at any and all ways to boost power, and settled on bolting an Eaton supercharger atop a cast-iron 4.6-liter block. New four-valve aluminum heads, forged connecting rods, crankshaft, and pistons, as well as an aluminum flywheel, helped the 390 horse-power survive harsh treatment. Though the coupe version started at $33,460, and the convertible at $37,835, it was a hit with buyers, as 13,476 vehicles were purchased.

Mustang fans rejoiced with the resurrection of the Mach 1 for 2003. With its 4.6-liter, 32-valve, dual-overhead-cam V-8 dishing out 305 horsepower, it could distance itself from the crowd with ease. The public ate the car up like free candy, with 9,652 sold. Ford originally intended the Mach 1 to be a one-year-only model, but the frenzied response by the public led FoMoCo to extend the car into the 2004 model year.

Every Mustang built for 2004 celebrated the Mustang's 40th anniversary with a badge on the front fender. Few would have believed in 1964 that the Mustang would still be available. Its competition had evaporated over the years, and now the original Pony Car was playing in a field of one. Yet its glory days were not over. An all-new Mustang was on the horizon, galloping hard for the showroom.

Ford engineers used a score of hot-rod tricks to coax 240 horsepower from the 5.0-liter EFI V-8.

The twin-cowl interior design hearkened back to the dual binnacle style of the original 1965 Mustang.

Each Mustang Cobra came with a set of Indy 500 decals in the trunk, to be put on at the new owner's discretion.

With the release of a fourth generation Mustang (SN95) in 1994, and the introduction of the SVT Cobra, the Mustang was chosen to once again pace the Indianapolis 500. A Cobra convertible using GT-40 heads, high lift 1.72:1 Crane rocker arms, a modified camshaft, and special fuel injectors, kept ahead of the race cars. Suspension mods unique to the Cobra included base V-6 front springs with a small anti-roll bar, and a beefy bar in the rear. Big 13.0-inch front brake rotors worked with 11.65-inch rear rotors to shed velocity.

A new lower front valance panel was special to the Cobra for 1994, which included integral foglamps.

Price: $25,605

Engine: 5.0L, 240-horsepower, 0-code, V-8

Transmission: 5-speed manual

Total Cobra Convertible production: 10,000

Since the days when Carroll Shelby affixed the Cobra logo on the sides of his modified Mustangs, the emblem has meant the strongest pony car available.

The color-shifting characteristics of the Mystic paint are evident on the hood. The scoops were non-functional.

Each Cobra engine was signed by the craftsmen that assembled it. The Cobra was 0.2 seconds faster to 60 miles per hour than the pushrod 5.0-liter.

Ford upped the horsepower ante in 1996 with a hefty infusion of grunt in the Cobra. Using a smaller 4.6-liter, DOHC V-8, the Mustang boasted of 305 horsepower under the long hood. As if the power increase wasn't enough, Cobra buyers could order a new paint color, Mystic, a spectacular color-changing finish that shifted between purple, green, and gold. Just the thing to stand out from the crowd.

Even though fuel economy standards were growing increasingly stringent, the 1996 Cobra enjoyed better fuel economy than previous years, while enjoying more power.

Price: $24,580

Engine: 4.6L, DOHC 305-horsepower, V-code V-8

Transmission: 5-speed manual

Total SVT Cobra Coupe production: 7,496

For the Mustang, 1997 was a year of mild evolution. A new anti-theft system became standard across the entire Mustang line, and 17-inch wheels became an option on the GT model. Over half of the Mustangs built in 1997 used the capable 150-horsepower, 3.8-liter V-6, but for power junkies, the 4.6-liter SOHC V-8 was the sure bet if a speeding ticket was on your list of must-do items.

The shoulder line on the Mustang GT was originally seen on the Mach III concept car from the early 1990s.

Price: $24,510

Engine: 4.6L, SOHC 215-horsepower, W-code V-8

Transmission: 4-speed automatic

Total GT coupe production: 18,464

The traditional Mustang pony seemed to float in the grille of the 1997 GT.

Above: In keeping with Mustang tradition, the taillights used a tri-element lens.

Left: Tasteful badging marked the engine displacement on the Mustang GT.

There was no need to put an engine badge on the side of the Cobra—it was understood that this was the strongest Mustang available.

The Cobra used PBR twin-piston calipers gripping 13.0-inch rotors in the front, while the 11.65-inch rear rotors used a single-piston caliper.

An aluminum block and heads helped hold the Cobra's weight down on the front tires. Torque was rated at 300 lb-ft at 4800 rpm.

"If it isn't broken, don't fix it" seemed to be Ford's manta for the 1998 Mustang Cobra. Still using the potent 4.6-liter DOHC V-8, it might not have been able to trounce the top-of-the-line Camaro and Firebird, but it was a winner where it really counted, in the showroom. While General Motors' F-body sold a total of 80,647 units, a whopping 175,522 Mustangs of all models went to good homes in 1998. A Cobra coupe tipped the scales at 3,391 pounds.

The Mustang Cobra's exterior differed from the GT model with the use of a different front bumper cover, rocker sill panels, and badging.

Price: $25,710

Engine: 4.6L, DOHC, 305-horsepower, V-code V-8

Transmission: 5-speed manual

Total Cobra coupe production: 5,174

A mild massaging of the exterior surfaces brought the Mustang into its 35th year, as crisper lines replaced the softer contours of prior years. A traction-control system became optional in 1999, and worked by cutting back engine power by retarding the spark and cutting fuel to cylinders when a wheel-slip sensor detected excessive tire rotation. A defeat button was provided for those inclined to abuse tires. Sub-frame connectors were used to minimize cowl shake.

Some of the styling cues used on the 1999 Mustang GT recalled the 1965 Mustang, including the faux scoop on the side and tri-element taillights.

Price: $24,870

Engine: 4.6L, SOHC, 260-horsepower, W-code V-8

Transmission: 4-speed automatic

Total GT convertible production: 13,669

Virtually every Mustang model has incorporated some sort of side body scoop, and the 1999 model was not exception.

With the 4.6-liter V-8, it wasn't hard to blur one's surroundings. Most contemporary magazines gave the nod to the Mustang for a superior ride over its competition.

Like the exterior, the cockpit benefited from a mild freshening, including new fabrics. The driver's seat was given one additional inch of travel.

The splitter is a race car–derived piece that can be removed for daily street use by twisting the Dzus fasteners and pulling the items away from the vehicle.

In the quarter-mile, the Cobra R could run the strip in 13.0 seconds at 108.5 miles per hour.

The heart of the Cobra R is the iron-block 5.4-liter DOHC V-8, topped by a plenum so large that the hood had to be bulged to provide clearance.

The Mustang came out looking for big game in 2000 with the release of the Cobra R, which was a thinly disguised race car legalized for use on the street. With a 385-horsepower, 5.4-liter DOHC V-8, six-speed manual transmission, independent rear suspension, and massive 265/40ZR-18 BF Goodrich g-Force tires, the Cobra R generated a 0 to 60 time of only 4.8 seconds. Devoid of air conditioning, radio or a back seat, it could hit 186 miles per hour right off the showroom floor. The exhaust system exited in front of the rear tires, a la the 1965 GT350, and at speed the roar was deafening, or music, depending on your point of view.

Not a vehicle for the timid or inexperienced, it didn't have any electronic traction control aids. The driver's right foot was the only traction control system.

Price: $55,000

Engine: 5.4L, DOHC 385-horsepower, H-code V-8

Transmission: 6-speed Tremec manual

Total Cobra R production: 300

Inside the huge 18-inch aluminum wheels are 14-inch rotors and 4-piston Alcon calipers in the front, and 13-inch rotors and 2-piston PBR calipers in the rear.

Roush installs a 6-psi Eaton supercharger, intercooler, high-flow intake, SVO heads, and SVO stainless steel headers to deliver 315 horsepower at the rear wheels.

The car is free, it's the badge that's expensive.

Master Ford wrench Jack Roush has forgotten more about Mustangs than most people know, and the Stage III setup shows just how well he can turn a wrench. From the Eaton supercharger atop the 4.6-liter V-8 to the beefed up suspension, brakes, and driveline, this is one of the most serious road machines wearing a galloping horse to ever roll down the pike. In the quarter-mile, it cracked out an E.T. of 13.56 seconds at 104.80 miles per hour. Sixty miles per hour came up in five seconds flat.

Subtle it's not. The Roush Mustang Stage III uses Ford tubular headers feeding a Flowmaster exhaust system that exits in front of the rear wheels. An interior roll bar helps to maintain structural rigidity.

Price: approx. $50,000

Engine: 4.6L SOHC, 315-horsepower, supercharged/intercooled V-8

Total 2001 Stage III production: 179

Ford had a full stable of Mustangs for 2001, and the GT soldiered on as the model delivering real performance value. Exterior changes included a non-functional hood scoop and rear wing that recalled the performance Mustangs of the late 1960s. Under the hood, the 4.6-liter V-8 continued to dish out healthy servings of horsepower (260) and torque (302 lb-ft), perfect for leaving long black lines on the tarmac. Traction control became standard in GT-models in 2001. Ford shuffled the option list to reduce the number of possible combinations from 2,600 to just 50.

For a platform over 20 years old, the 2001 Mustang GT has enjoyed constant refinement. Cruising down Pacific Coast Highway at sunset with the top down is reason enough to own a Mustang convertible.

Price: $26,885

Engine: 4.6L, 260-horsepower, SOHC, X-code V-8

Transmission: 4-speed automatic

Total Mustang GT convertible production: 18,336

Yet another variation on the three-element tail-light, the 2001 Mustang returned to a vertical motif and large lenses.

Instrumentation on the 2001 Mustang GT was clear and easy to read. The beefy V-8 could coax the speedometer needle into the upper range of the dial.

All 2001 Mustangs fitted the Center High Mounted Stop Light (CHMSL) in the trailing edge of the trunk lid.

The Bullitt concept car was unveiled at the 2000 Los Angeles Auto Show to critical acclaim.

A brushed-aluminum fuel filler door was one of the discrete styling touches that made the 2001 Bullitt Mustang special.

One of the most appreciated upgrades unique to the 2001 Bullitt package was the fitting of Brembo brakes, shortening stopping distances and improving brake feel.

Years after the Steve McQueen movie *Bullitt* had played in theaters, Ford introduced the Bullitt-model Mustang in 2001, complete with an aggressive soundtrack and modern Torq-Thrust look wheels. While the vehicle could be had in True Blue and Black, most buyers lived out their silver-screen fantasies in a Highland Green version. Using a cast aluminum intake manifold, twin 57-millimeter throttle bodies, and high-flow mufflers helped to raise the horsepower by 10, and the lowered suspension aided in delivering crisper handling. The Bullitt Mustang was a one-year only model, and it roared straight into America's heart.

The Bullitt Package was $3,695 more than the price of a GT model, but one of the things it bought was exclusivity.

Price: $26,830

Engine: 4.6L, 270-horsepower, SOHC, X-code V-8

Transmission: 5-speed manual

Total Bullitt production: 5,582

Most of the ink spread on Mustangs has covered the high-performance V-8 models. Yet the majority of Mustangs built over the years have had a six-cylinder engine under the hood. The 2002 model was typical of most, delivering good fuel economy with peppy performance, while attractively priced. The EPA rated the V-6 manual transmission model at 20-miles per gallon/city, 29-miles per gallon/highway. Like all 2002 Mustangs, it used MacPherson struts and lower A-arms in the front suspension and a live axle in the rear.

At a quick glance, the V-6 Mustang could be mistaken for the muscular GT model. With a curb weight of only 3,064 pounds, the V6 variant enjoyed spirited handling.

Price: $17,475

Engine: 3.8L, 193-horsepower, 4-code V-6

Transmission: 5-speed manual standard

Total V-6 coupe production: 67,090

Starting in 2001, 16-inch wheels became standard on the V-6 Mustang. Many prefer the clean lines of the base Mustang over the flashier GT.

Like all Mustangs since 1965, the side scoops have been for show only. The original 1962 Mustang I used a rear mid-engine configuration, hence the side scoops.

A clean grille was one of the styling hallmarks that the V-6 Mustang shared with its pricier V-8 stablemate.

A storied name in Mustang circles returned in 2003 as Ford's Living Legends program reintroduced the Mach 1. Complete with a "Shaker" hood, spoilers, and stripes, it vividly recalled the 1969–1970 Mach 1. The interior was done up in "Comfortweave" leather, and the instrument panel used a font reminiscent of years gone past. Under the hood, a 4.6-liter, 32-valve, V-8 cranked out 310 horsepower with the manual transmission, 308 when bolted to an automatic. Horsepower came back with a vengeance. Ford improved the front impact safety structure, earning the Mustang a five-star rating.

The 2003 Mustang Mach 1 boasted a functional Shaker hood scoop that fed outside air to the inductions system.

Price: $28,705

Engine: 4.6L, 310-horsepower, DOHC, R-code V-8

Transmission: 5-speed manual

Total Mach 1 production: 9,652

The Mach 1 returned in 2003, featuring a lowered (1/2-inch) suspension and firmer springs and aggressively turned shock absorbers.

Modeled on the scoop from the 1969 Mach 1, the 2003 version shook when the engine was revved, and helped to deliver 320 lb-ft of torque.

Ford has used the dual cowl design in the Mustang's interior since 1965, and the 2003 Mach 1 carried the tradition forward.

Above left: Each member of the engine's two-man assembly team signed the huge valve cover before the vehicle hit the showroom.

Above right: This is what the 2003 Cobra is made to do, blur the world. Giant Goodyear Eagle F1 GS tires (P275/40ZR17) were mounted at each corner, helping to maintain a grip.

Right: The not-inexpensive Cobra used upscale materials to differentiate it from its regular Mustang cousins.

Mustang buyers in 2003 were blessed with so many variants to choose from. Top dog in the field was the powerful Cobra, now packing a DOHC, V-8 under the graceful hood. Between the top of the engine and the bottom of the hood is a belt-driven supercharger; it goes a long way to help deliver 390 honest horsepower. A boost gauge in the interior helped the driver monitor pressure into the engine, while huge 13-inch discs in the front and 11.65-inch rotors in the rear helped slow the beast down. Top speed was 155 miles per hour.

Part of the Cobra package was the ability to cover the quarter-mile in only 13.12 seconds at 109.6 miles per hour.

Price: $37,780

Engine: 4.6L, 390-horsepower, supercharged, DOHC, Y-code V-8

Transmission: 6-speed manual

Total Cobra production: 13,476

Price: **NA**

Engine: **4.6L, 400-horsepower, supercharged, DOHC V-8**

Transmission: **5-speed automatic**

Total Concept production: **2**

When the new Mustang Concept was unveiled at the 2003 North American International Auto Show, the public and the press were stunned. Ford stylists assured the public that the concept car was 90 to 95 percent accurate at depicting what the production Mustang would look like. With massive 20-inch wheels enveloping 13.8-inch Brembo brakes, and a 400-horsepower engine under the long hood, it used familiar Mustang styling cues on a modern platform, creating the best of both worlds.

Painted Redline Metallic, the convertible shared the spotlight with a Tungsten Silver coupe.

One change that was made from concept to production was the insertion of six inches of length between the firewall and the front wheel centers to enlarge the engine compartment and give the car better proportions.

Cluster gauges featured round, optical-inspired faces to present information and impart a "heritage" feel.

Ford used a 5-speed automatic transmission in their functional 2005 Mustang Concept vehicle.

Price: $33,440

Engine: 4.6L, 390-horsepower, supercharged, DOHC, Y-code V-8

Transmission: 6-speed manual

Total Cobra (coupe/convertible) production: 5,664

When the driver buries the accelerator in the Cobra, they had better have the car pointed in the right direction. With 390 horsepower and 390 lb-ft of twist, it was easy to use your right foot to steer. Mystichrome paint was offered, a $3,650 option, and it included a leather-covered steering wheel and seats that used the color-changing technology. A no-cost rear spoiler delete option was available.

Not a car for the driver wanting to remain inconspicuous, a Mystichrome Cobra with chromed wheels was a stylish way to get from A to B.

Car and Driver magazine blurred the pavement at a drag strip, covering the distance in 12.9 seconds at 112 miles per hour.

With the top two gears in the 6-speed manual transmission overdrive ratios, it's possible to attain 22-miles per gallon on the freeway.

Ford used a cast-iron block for durability in the 2004 Cobra, but the heads and intake were aluminum.

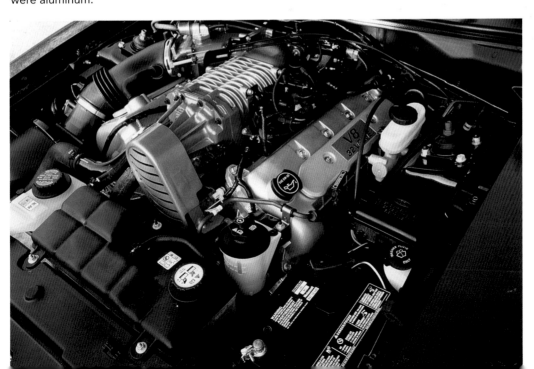

Ford saw the SN-95 platform go out on a high note with the 2004 Mustang GT. Every Mustang built in 2004 wore a "40th Anniversary" badge on its front fenders, and for a modest $175, the Sport Appearance Package delivered Arizona Beige Metallic accents on the hood, lower rocker panels upgraded wheels with Arizona Beige Metallic inserts. For the sonically-inclined, the $550 Mach 460 sound system included a 6-disc CD changer and enough watts to push the Mustang down the road.

The Mustang GT had the muscle car landscape all to itself by 2004 with the demise of the Camaro and Firebird.

Price: $24,850

Engine: 4.6L, 260-horsepower, SOHC, X-code V8

Transmission: 5-speed manual

Total 2004 Mustang production: 141,907

Four-wheel disc brakes help to haul the Mustang GT down from its 140-miles-per-hour top speed.

Gracing the fender of every 2004 Mustang, the 40th Anniversary badging follows Ford's tradition of celebrating every 5th birthday of the Mustang.

Recalling the handsome hood scoops of Mustangs past, the 2004 GT model's hood wore a large non-functional scoop.

2005-Beyond

Chapter 7

When the 2005 Mustang was finally revealed at the 2003 North American International Auto Show, it was the culmination of years of work. It was essentially a fresh-sheet design.

J. Mays, Ford group vice president of design, worked with designer Doug Gaffka to research early Mustangs to determine what visual cues should be incorporated in the new design. They realized that when most people thought of "classic" Mustangs, the 1965–1970 era came most strongly to mind. This was the source of the bulk of styling cues. As Mays recounts to Matt DeLorenzo in his book *Mustang: A New Breed of Pony Car*, "The trick to all these cars that have a heritage to them is that you actually create two or three focal points and leave a lot of blank space in between. The whole idea is leaving the big blank spaces and having a couple of cues where people say 'Oh yeah, I get it,' and let them fill in the blanks. This allows the car to

resonate with people because it is filled with their own personal meaning".

The result was a pair of body styles, a fastback coupe and a convertible. One of the most prominent Mustang cues is the long hood/short deck proportions that the original Mustang popularized. A C-pillar window, lifted off of the 1966 Shelby GT350, is another of the most identifiable stylistic flourishes used. With two engines offered, a 4.0-liter V-6 and a 4.6-liter V-8, designers used a couple of elements to quickly visually differentiate vehicles using one engine or the other. Mustang GTs had a spoiler mounted on the trunk lid, and large fog lamps were incorporated into the grille. Vehicles using the V-6 had a lampless grille and no tail spoiler. But the differences were more than skin deep. Ford put a lot of thought into each powertrain, and the effort paid off.

Many times in the Mustang's history, the base engine was barely able to get the vehicle out of its own way. That situation changed dramatically with the introduction of the 4.0-liter, 60-degree V-6 in the 2005 model. Rated at 210 horsepower, their single overhead cam designs allowed it to breathe properly right up to its 6,100-rpm redline. With a torque peak of 240 lb-ft at 3,500 rpm, it could step off sharply from the line. Ford execs expected the product mix to be 2/3 six-cylinder equipped cars, the remaining 1/3 outfitted as GTs.

As the top engine on the Mustang menu, the 4.6-liter V-8 had to perform strongly right out of the box. With a rating of 300 horsepower at 6,000 rpm, and 315 lb-ft of torque at 4,500 revs, the three-valve, SOHC engine was a powerplant born to rev. This engine was the first in Mustang history to use electronic throttle control, its computer reading the signal from the primary sensor located at the accelerator pedal and matching it to information regarding engine speed and load, cam timing, and the fuel injection system.

All that power had to go somewhere, and the live rear axle was designed to put the grunt to the ground. A modified three-link affair, it used a Panhard rod that increased torsional stiffness to prevent rear-end hop under hard cornering. The rod acted to prevent lateral movement during the full range of motion the axle might encounter in use. This allowed stiffer bushings to be used, minimizing steering deflection under load, as well as reducing unsprung weight, aiding handling. Front and rear stabilizer bars helped in keeping maximum rubber on the road, while keeping body roll to a minimum.

All of these bits and pieces were attached to a body structure that was 31 percent stiffer in torsional rigidity than the 2004 model. Having a stiff body structure allowed for a more athletic suspension without the sacrifice of ride comfort. The interior was a new design as well, with a twin-cowl design that echoed the 1965 Mustang.

In the summer of 2006, Ford's latest high performance Mustang hit showrooms, the GT500. Performance legend Carroll Shelby teamed up with Ford Motor Company again to develop the Ford GT supercar, then assisted in creating the modern version of his late-1960s GT350s and GT500s. With an intercooled supercharger atop a 5.4-liter iron block/aluminum head V-8 that was essentially a barely de-tuned Ford GT engine, it stickered for $39,995. Rated at more than 450 horsepower and 450 lb-ft of torque, it was the performance bargain of the year.

The 2007 GT500 was not the only Mustang that Carroll Shelby blessed. In 1965, Shelby fitted a Paxton belt-driven supercharger on a prototype GT350, coaxing upwards of 100 more horsepower from the 289-ci V-8.

Unfortunately for performance enthusiasts, Ford pulled the plug on SVT, shuttering the division on April 1, 2006. Ford Motor Company announced the "Way Forward" plan, in an effort to halt the loss of market share and its accompanying fiscal woes. Some executives felt that pursuing high performance ran counter to corporate goals, so a case was made to shut down the long-running group. Only time will tell if the decision was the right one.

Price: $29,565

Engine: 4.6L, 300-horsepower, SOHC, V8

Transmission: 5-speed manual

Total GT convertible production: N/A

The all-new 2005 Mustang was a runaway hit, using scores of familiar Mustang styling cues to create a modern version of a classic. Built at Flat Rock, Michigan, the suspension utilizes MacPherson struts with coil-over springs in the front and a three-link live rear axle equipped with a Panhard rod to minimize lateral axle movement. The convertible was designed alongside the coupe, thus it enjoys considerably more structurally rigidity than its predecessors.

An aggressive stance helps the 2005 Mustang exude menace. Covered headlights are a Mustang first.

Classic "long hood/short deck" proportions are pure pony car styling cues, and the 2005 Mustang wears them well.

Above: As per standard Mustang, the rear seats are diminutive, ideal for children and groceries.

Left: The hooded dashboard recalls the dash of the 1965 Mustang, while the instrument panel used the 1968 'Stang as its inspiration.

Price: $19,570

Engine: 4.0L, 210-horsepower, SOHC, V-6

Transmission: 5-speed manual

Total production: N/A

Ford estimates that the V-6 Mustang accelerates to 60 miles per hour in 7 seconds when equipped with a manual transmission, 7.5 with the five-speed automatic. A quick way to tell if an oncoming Mustang has a V-6 or V-8 powerplant is to glance at the grille. The V-8 models sport a pair of inboard fog lamps in the grille opening, while V-6-motivated Mustangs lack the lamps. Unlike some prior years' Mustangs, the current base engine provides plenty of grunt, while delivering 19/28 miles per gallon, city/highway, when fitted with the manual tranny. The V-6 Mustang is electronically limited to 112 miles per hour.

Clean lines and trim proportions are Mustang hallmarks, and the V-6 powered version is very easy on the eyes—and the wallet, starting at $19,570.

Full-sized drivers fit easily behind the handsome steering wheel, as the 107.1-inch wheelbase allowed the stylists to provide plenty of interior space.

Base V-6 Mustangs use 16-inch, 10-spoke alloy wheels with simulated knock-off spinners.

The 4.0-liter V-6 packs 240 lb-ft of torque, more than enough to smoke the rear tires. The engine is essentially the same one used in the Explorer, but uses a different intake manifold.

With 300 horsepower and 315 lb-ft of torque for under $27K, the 2005 Mustang has been embraced as the performance buy of the year. With a three-valve cylinder head configuration and an electronic throttle, the response is startling to the first-timer behind the wheel. A very rigid body structure (31 percent stiffer than 2004) ensures that the advanced suspension can maintain proper wheel geometry under almost any condition. Zero to 60 miles per hour takes around 5.2 seconds, while the quarter-mile can be covered in 13.90 seconds at 104 miles per hour. Top speed is 143 miles per hour.

Price (GT Deluxe): $24,370

Engine: 4.6L, 300-horsepower, SOHC, V-8

Transmission: 5-speed automatic

Total production: N/A

Ford realizes that the appearance of the engine is important, thus considerable attention was paid to the 4.6-liter V-8 found under the hood of the Mustang GT.

The rear "filler" on the 2005 Mustang is really a faux cap, evoking the fuel filler from earlier years. The functional fuel filler is located on the side of the vehicle.

From its aggressive front end to the tri-element taillights, the 2005 Mustang oozes high-performance.

While the headlights are covered on the 2006 Mustang GT, the stylists incorporated the "gills" found on the 1965 Mustang.

Low profile tires help the 2006 Mustang GT find its way around a corner like a slot car, yet provide a firm but comfortable ride.

Straightforward, attractive and strong, the 4.6-liter V-8 uses twin throttle bodies to help the engine quickly reach its 5,750 rpm redline.

Ford continued the home run streak in 2006 with the Mustang, introducing two new colors and the V-6 Pony Package. Buyers ordering a GT with the manual transmission got a 3.55:1 limited slip rear axle ration, while automatic transmission customers filled the differential with a 3.31:1 gearset. For Mustang owners wanting a slightly lower profile, the rear wing could be deleted from the factory. Fuel economy was rated at 17/25 miles per gallon with V-8 and manual transmission. Stainless steel functional dual exhaust is standard on the GT model.

Tungsten Grey Clearcoat Metallic is one of the two new colors for Model Year 2006. This is the same color as the Mustang Concept Coupe.

Price (GT Premium): $26,320

Engine: 4.6L, 300-horsepower, SOHC, V-8

Transmission: 5-speed manual

Total production: N/A

While the interior uses many styling cues from earlier Mustangs, the 2006 version is a clean, fresh design.

Thanks to technology, it's now possible to get neck-snapping power and 25 miles per gallon on the highway.

The current car is the first production Mustang with covered headlights, while the inboard fog lamps recall first generation 'Stangs.

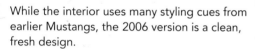

Ford continued to hone the latest Mustang for 2006 with new colors and options. While the biggest news for 2006 Mustang fans was the release of the Pony Package, a dress-up option for V-6-equipped 'Stangs, the beefy V-8 GT continued to grab headlines and sales. *Car and Driver* magazine voted it America's Best Muscle Car, and with its 320 lb-ft of torque and live rear axle, it's as easy to steer with the throttle as the steering wheel. From the aggressive front end to the *Bullitt*-inspired exhaust burble, the current GT convertible is an outstanding way to let ones cares blow away in the breeze.

Four different wheel/tire combinations are available on the GT model, including two 18-inch wheels. *Photos courtesy of Mike Mueller*

Price: $29,965

Engine: 4.6L, OHC, 300-horsepower V-8

Transmission: 5-speed automatic

Production: N/A

Price: $39,995 (est.)

Engine: 5.4L, 475-horsepower, supercharged, DOHC V-8

Transmission: 6-speed manual

Total production: N/A

Ford and Carroll Shelby collaborated to create the GT500, bringing back one of the most storied names in Mustang history. Like prior Shelby Mustangs, the GT500 pushes the performance and styling envelope, resulting in a serious driver's car. This is not a machine for the timid or shy, as its throaty roar under full throttle, and scenery-blurring abilities test anyone's self-restraint. A leather-heavy interior provides a comfortable setting for throttle-heavy fun.

Designed by SVT, Ford's in-house go-fast division, it is a direct threat to the Corvette.

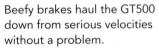

Beefy brakes haul the GT500 down from serious velocities without a problem.

Hunkered down for speed, the GT500 is the picture of an aggressive muscle car. SVT engineers designed it to corner and stop as well as it accelerates.

A belt-driven screw-type supercharged pushes air into the 32-valve heads, while stainless-steel dual exhaust system directs burnt hydrocarbons to the vehicles wake.